THE SCIENCE
OF MOTIVATION

THE SCIENCE
OF MOTIVATION

Strategies and Techniques for Turning Dreams into Destiny

BRIAN TRACY
with DAN STRUTZEL

gildanpress

gildanpress

Published 2017 by Gildan Press
an imprint of Gildan Media LLC.
Copyright © 2017 by Brian Tracy

Distributed through the Book market by Hachette Book Group, USA

First Edition: 2017

Front Cover design: Cindy Joy

Interior design by Meghan Day Healey of Story Horse, LLC.

Library of Congress Cataloging-in-Publication Data
is available upon request

ISBN: 978-1-469-03572-7

Manufactured in the United States of America by LSC Communications

10   9   8   7   6   5   4   3   2   1

CONTENTS

FOREWORD

The Dynamic Conversations Series

Brian Tracy is one of the world's foremost authorities on business and personal success. He has given more than 5000 talks and seminars to over five million people and is a business coach to top leaders in major industries worldwide.

Dan Strutzel is a 25-year veteran of the personal development industry, publishing some of the most successful audio programs in history. He has worked up close and personally with most of the top personal development authors and speakers.

Dan was thrilled when Brian agreed to sit down together to discuss his seminar *The Science of Motivation*. Meeting over the course of a long weekend, these thinkers were able to explore this topic deeply and at great length. These in-depth interviews were taped and are presented here. We hope you enjoy and benefit from their discussion.

ONE

Why Is Motivation So Important?

Dan

The legendary college football coach and analyst Lou Holtz once said, "When all is said and done, more is said than done." These simple yet extremely profound words explain one of the biggest predicaments that individuals face today. Many of us say we want to be successful, happy, and influential. Yet very few of us follow up what we say with specific actions that move us directly toward those goals.

The idea of being successful is an attractive dream that fills us with positive emotions, whereas the actions required to be successful at work, in our relationships, in sports, are often difficult and lengthy. The desire to be genuinely happy is a universal goal to which nearly every individual aspires, but the actions required to achieve deep and sustained happiness—some call it joy—often require us to delay temporary gratification and avoid quick fixes to problems.

Saying that we want to achieve a level of influence, either as a leader of others in the workplace, an influential member of the community, or as an admired parent and spouse, is far easier than the gut-wrenching decisions, enormous amounts of personal time, and direct truth-telling that are required. This gap between what we say we want and what we must do to achieve it can often feel as large and distant and mysterious as a black hole. It separates those who are able to turn their dreams into their destiny from those who aren't.

What do we need to do to bridge this gap between what we say we want and what we must do to achieve it? We need goal-oriented motivation. This specific kind of motivation is the fuel that takes us across the long and often uncertain bridge to our desired destination in life. What would it mean for you to learn how to develop this kind of motivation on demand, sustain this motivation through the difficult periods of life, and instill it so intricately into your daily life that you make the very idea of motivation unnecessary?

All of that and more is available to you in this all-new cutting-edge book, *The Science of Motivation: Strategies and Techniques for Turning Dreams into Destiny* from personal development expert and motivation master Brian Tracy.

Here you'll learn that the typical ideas of motivation as something that comes and goes, often out of your control, like a balloon being filled with air from the outside in, are completely inaccurate. Motivation has been studied, as have the methods and strategies needed to replicate it. Truly, there is a science of motivation and, as with any other subject which has been scientifically studied and tested, if you implement its causes in your life, you will and must produce the effects and move toward the outcomes that you desire.

After clearing away the numerous myths about motivation, Brian will present and discuss this cutting-edge science with you.

If you apply it systematically to your life, your dreams will become your destiny.

In this first part we're going to talk about why motivation is so important. There's an idea out there that talent, brains, and education are what you need to be successful in this world. There's a lot of talk about having the right kind of education—for example, STEM education: science, technology, engineering, and math. If you do, you'll be successful in your career moving forward. Or if somebody gets the right score on the ACT or SAT test and has the right brains. Or just a great talent, whether it's something that they've developed as a prodigy or something that they've worked on. There is the idea that these things are sufficient for success.

How do you feel about that and where does motivation come in?

Brian

I started off my life quite humbly. I didn't graduate from high school, and I worked at laboring jobs. The first job I got was washing dishes in the back of a small hotel. All the time I was growing up I received, unfortunately, no motivation aside from threats and punishment from my parents and my family. I was told that if you don't get a good education, you won't be successful. If you don't get a good education, you won't go to college. You won't get a good job, you won't marry well, and you'll just have to struggle. This is used as a threat to encourage people to do better as students.

However, what I absorbed is that if I didn't get a good education, then I've missed the boat and all I could do is laboring jobs. And that's what I did. I worked at a variety of laboring jobs, and my only thought was "I didn't graduate from high school, so I'll just seek out more laboring jobs." I worked in sawmills. I worked in the brush with a chain saw. I worked on farms, on ranches. I worked in factories. I worked in sawmills stacking lumber. I worked digging ditches. All basically Joe jobs, minimum wage jobs. The minimum wage was much lower than it is today.

I kept believing this. When I could no longer find a laboring job because of the economy, I got a job making sales, 100% commission, working from door to door. I worked at that for months and months. Then I had a turning point in my life. I'll never forget it.

I noticed that one of the guys in our office who was selling the same product out of the same office was earning ten times as much as anyone else, and he wasn't even working very hard. I was getting up at 6:00 in the morning and preparing. I was out there knocking on doors when people came to work at 8:00 or 8:30. I'd knock on office and industrial doors all day long. At night I'd go out and knock on apartment doors and on doors in the residential neighborhoods. I'd maybe make one sale all day.

This guy made four or five sales a day, and he'd start at 9:30. He'd quit at 4:30, go out for lunch, and went to nightclubs. He always had lots of money, and he was only about three or four years older than me. He was pretty casual. He didn't seem like a genius. He was just a nice guy.

I went and I asked him, "Why are you so much more successful than I am?" He said, "Show me your sales process and I'll critique it for you." I said, "I don't have a sales process." He said, "A sales process is like a recipe or a success formula. If you don't have one, you're simply not going to be successful in preparing a dish or getting results." He showed me his sales process.

It was pretty basic: when you meet a prospect, you just ask them questions.

But when I met a prospect, I would talk at them as fast as I could to try to get them interested in my product before they shut down and told me, "I've got to get back to work. Leave it with me and I'll look it over." He said, "No, no, no. You have to separate prospects from suspects. You have to ask questions to find out if this person can actually use our product."

I began to ask questions, and I started to get better results. I went back to him, and I said, "What else can you do?" He said, "Have you read any books on sales?" Books on sales? I had no idea there were books on sales. I went down to the bookstore, and I started to buy and read every book from cover to cover and underline in them.

Then I heard about audio programs on sales. Those were cassettes at the time, and I began to listen to audio cassettes every spare minute when I was walking around. Between calls I would listen to an audio cassette on sales. Then I'd go in to see a person and I'd put it aside and remember what I learned on the cassette and I would try it out.

Then I went to my first sales seminar. I learned two things here. Number one is that all success skills are learnable. You can learn any skill you need to learn to achieve any goal you can set for yourself. Before that time, I thought that my life was pretty much fated for underachievement, because all I'd ever done was work at laboring jobs and get fired. I slept on the street and in my car. I slept on the floor at friends' apartments. Suddenly I realized that your destiny is in your own hands, that you can learn any skill you need to learn. This motivated me then, and it motivates me now.

Whenever I see a subject that's of some interest to me, I pounce on it. Today, when I go onto Amazon, I find the highest rated books on the subject or the books that are recommended. I get them and read them from cover to cover, underlining. Then because I'm a teacher, a speaker and a presenter, I start to incorporate these ideas into my seminars. My audiences come up to me and say, "Geez, I never thought of that before; that is a great idea."

One of my clients in Stockholm came back to me one year later. He said, "That one idea in your business seminar has enabled us to increase our business fifteen times in the last twelve months in a very competitive market. We just changed the whole focus of our business, as you recommended, to getting more and more referrals from happy customers. That meant to go and look at every single piece of our business, every activity, to make sure that every single customer was extremely happy, so happy they would spontaneously bring their friends. After years of being in business, we grew our business fifteen times. We're exploding with that one idea from your seminar. I paid $500 for it, and it's been worth millions to us."

Study after study has been done at Harvard and other universities about natural intelligence, excellent grades, and so on. None of them have any correlation with success. There are people who came to this country with no degrees, no language skills, no money, no nothing, and today they're millionaires. There are people who came from the wealthiest homes who are driving taxis. There are people who grew up on farms who own their own multinational businesses. There's no correlation at all between education, skills, family, or even luck. It's all self-determined by the individual. Every individual has within their abilities the capability of accomplishing extraordinary things. They just have to learn how to do it.

Dan

Just to build on that then, Brian, would you say that, paradoxically, if you have all the talent in the world, you're looked at as this prodigy, you've gone to the best school, that could serve to take away that key motivation that might inspire someone who doesn't have those things?

Brian

It's very much like coming from a family where nutrition and exercise are not thought about or talked about: you'll end up eating the wrong foods. When our kids were growing up, we never had Cokes or soft drinks in our home, and we exercised all the time. We have exercise equipment. We go for walks. We swim. We read all the time. Our kids are seeing that this is the norm: you read a lot, you exercise a lot, and you eat good foods. We didn't have to lecture to them; we just didn't give them an alternative. Their friends started to put on weight drinking Cokes and eating candy, cake, and everything else.

Your initial environment is extremely important, but your initial environment does not determine your future. You can throw that off.

One thing I learned that has transformed my thinking is the centrality of what is called the *self-concept*. The self-concept is the way you think about yourself, feel about yourself, see yourself. On the outside, you always perform consistently with the person that you think you are on the inside. The starting point of all performance change is to change your self-concept so that you realize you can do vastly more than you've ever done before.

My friend Denis Waitley has this wonderful line: "You have more potential than you could use in a hundred lifetimes." I remember when I was twenty-one years old, and struggling, I came across a book on the works of psychologist Abraham Maslow, and I read it from cover to cover. Basically it says that the average individual has extraordinary potential. We don't use 10% of our potential, as is commonly said. We use more like 2% of our potential.

The potential you have is extraordinary, and as Denis says, you couldn't use it all in a hundred lifetimes. How do you get that potential out? You simply delve deep into it by learning and practicing new things.

Your self-concept is initially formed by the way your parents treat you. Whenever you see an unhappy adult, you see a bad childhood. Whenever you see a dysfunctional adult, you see a dysfunctional childhood. There is a line from Alexander Pope, the English poet, who said, "As a twig is bent the tree is inclined," which means that when you're a twig, when you're young, if you're bent toward negativity, as you get older you'll get more and more negative. It's the way you think about yourself and your possibilities that, more than anything else, determines your successes.

However, at a certain point, it's your turn to drive. You slip behind the wheel of your own car, and you can decide where you're going to go mentally. You can decide the thoughts that you're going to think, and even how you're going to think them, and how you're going to interpret things. Nothing that occurred in your past can have any influence over you except the influence that you allow it to have.

Martin Seligman's work had a profound effect on my thinking. He found that optimism is the most important predictor of success and happiness in life. Optimism can be measured in a basic test, and then it can be measured and remeasured to determine if you're becoming more and more optimistic.

Here are three questions we sometimes ask at the beginning of my special seminars. The questions are simple, but they're used by the largest consultant agencies in America working with senior executives to get a picture of what's going on in a person's head.

The first is this: complete the sentence "I am." What words that come to your mind when you say I am? Because that describes your self-image, your self-concept, your self-valuation, and a lot of other things.

Some people would describe themselves by saying, "I am a happy person, a good father or mother, an excellent worker with tremendous and unlimited potential." That's a really good self-concept to have, because it will give you the energy and the power to overcome almost any adversity. Other people will say negative things. "I'm an average person and I have nothing but problems and difficulties, and I keep on hanging in there believing that things will get better." Two different worldviews—and everybody's got a worldview.

The second question we ask is "Describe people." The best ones say, "People are interesting. People are amazing. People are so different. People are fascinating." They'll talk about people in the most positive terms. The people who carry placards and riot in the streets will say, "People are no good. They're always out to take advantage of you. People are crooks." They have a negative view of people.

The third question we ask is "What is life?" You'll find that most of our social problems come from the bottom 80%—people who think that life is oppressive and unfair and that incomes are unfairly unequal. They talk about the 1% versus the 99% and say that life is full of people taking advantage of you.

But all of the successful people in my programs say, "Life is wonderful. It's a great adventure. It sure beats the alternative. It's getting better and better. It's under your control." Those world-views determine which direction your life is going to go in.

Here's the wonderful thing. At any time in your life, you can choose to change your direction, just as you can wrench the wheel of your car and take a different road. Every major change in a person's life comes when their mind collides with a new idea. The new idea, is that *you can do anything you put your mind to.*

I was listening to a very successful multimillionaire. She was worth more than $100 million, a woman who finds, develops, and retail markets products in ventures; she's on *Shark Tank*. She was asked what her philosophy is. She said, "My parents always told me I could do anything in the world, that there was no limit on what I could accomplish. I grew up absolutely believing that, and it turned out to be true."

Dan

That's great. I love that. Now there's another aspect of this: society, and in particular the media, often serve to demotivate us. They work on the premise that bad news sells and crisis sells. Even outside the media, amongst our peer group, there are people around us who will try to tear us down when we're trying to be success-ful, trying to do something original, extraordinary. They'll say, "What are you trying to do? Why are you going to risk all that?"

There does seem to be an aspect of our society that is putting out all the wrong messages, serving to pull people back to the average. Talk about that impact, and why it's so important that we create an environment to motivate ourselves.

Brian

In my earlier programs I've talked about the power of suggestion and the power of the suggestive influences around you. Of course, the people closest to you have the greatest power of suggestion or influence: your family, your children, and so on. Then there are your coworkers and your boss and, as you go further out, society. One thing I would preach is control your suggestive environment. It's almost like the emotional and mental pool in which you swim.

Rich people watch an average of one hour of television each day, roughly, and it's either prerecorded or carefully selected. Poor people watch five to seven hours of television, and they watch whatever is on. Now as you said, if it bleeds, it leads. In the news business, what really gets viewers—which enables them to sell advertising—is dramatic stuff.

We can take as an example, a presidential candidate who has massive news coverage every single day because he says completely outrageous things over and over, and he is great copy. He appears and makes himself available for any interview on radio, television, newspapers, much more than any of the other candidates, so he gets lots of exposure. He gets on there, and he says outrageous things. People watch it, and the media sell the advertising.

People are greatly influenced by their milieus, by the news, by what's going on around them. If you do not have a clear sense of yourself, a clear center, you can be easily influenced by all the negative stuff that you hear.

If you get down to the bottom line, we are still living in the best time in all of human history. We can live longer. We can live better. We can live healthier. We have more choices. Of course, we have a lot of problems, but one of the great rules for me—and I read this over and over from other successful people—is never worry about things you can't do anything about. You cannot change many of the negative parts of our society. All you can do is change yourself. Albert Jay Nock, one of the great thinkers of the last century, said, "Each one improve one. Your major business in life is to present society with one improved unit, yourself, and if you make yourself better by that very action you raise the entire average of your entire society and that is completely under your control." What a great guiding influence! The more you get better and better at what you do, the better job and better work you do, the better you treat other people, the more, in your own little way, you raise the entire average of the society you live in.

Dan

Focus on your individual unit; in many ways, that's the best service you can be to society.

As we go through life, no matter how well things are going, life is going to throw challenges at us to take us off track. A big part of motivation is to make a decision ahead of time about how we're going to react to certain challenges when they're presented—even things that we can't anticipate. How can you create a mind-set so that a challenge doesn't so depress you? An unexpected person passes away, or your business is hit with a major challenge. Can you preset your mind so that you can make it through those challenges more easily and remain motivated?

Brian

You have to quickly separate things that are under your control from things that aren't. We cannot control the Zika virus, and we can't control acts of terrorism in Brussels and Paris. These are things we can't do anything about. We can't control whether a loved one passes away. The only thing that we can control is ourselves. We can control our own emotions. We can control our own thoughts.

Now let us say that we're in a business crisis. The market goes down. The competition comes up with something that's twice as good and half the price, which happens far too often now.

There *is* something that under your control, there is something you can do something about. What you do is you accept responsibility.

I spent 4000 hours studying positive emotions. I came across some work that was started in 1895. I came across this concept. It said that basically everyone wants to be happy, as you said earlier. So why aren't people happy? Well, the block between where you are today and your happiness is always negative emotions of some kind, a negative self-concept, a negative idea. It's negative emotions.

Negative emotions all come down to anger, either inwardly expressed—you're angry with yourself, which makes you feel inferior and insecure and not very happy with your life—or outwardly expressed. You express it to others. You blow up, you criticize, you condemn, you are down on other people. You feel that you're oppressed, you make demonstrations against the successful, and so on. These feelings of anger always come down to one thing. It's called *blame*. Blame is the essential reason for all negative emotions. If you stop blaming, the negative emotions stop simultaneously.

How do you stop blaming? It's very simple. You simply accept responsibility. You see, your mind can only hold one thought at a time, positive or negative. If you accept responsibility by saying the magic words *I am responsible, I am responsible, I am responsible*, then you instantly stop all negative emotions, because you cannot accept responsibility and be negative simultaneously.

If you do something over and over again, you develop a habit. Soon you develop a habit of accepting responsibility for any difficulty in your life—of which there will be an endless number—and then taking action and doing whatever you can do. If something happens to someone in your family, the next question is "I am responsible for this or that or something else; what actions can I take?" Then take those actions.

Because you can only think of one thing at a time, when you take action of any kind, you forget instantly about all the negative emotions. You cannot be acting and thinking negatively at the same time. That's why the best cure for worry is continuous action in the direction of your goal. The best way to eliminate any negative feeling is to accept responsibility, and then get busy.

Theodore Roosevelt had this beautiful line. He said, "Do what you can with what you have, right where you are." The only point you can control is this moment. Do what you can with what you have, right where you are. Accept responsibility and take action, and positive emotions will replace the negative emotions, because nature abhors a vacuum. If you can get rid of negative emotions, you become a completely positive person. If you repeat the process over and over again, pretty soon you're basically a happy person all the time. You don't have any negative emotion. You're not angry with anybody. It doesn't mean that you don't disagree or disapprove of certain behaviors, but you're not angry.

You'll find that people who are in control of their own emotions may disagree, but they're not disagreeable. This is the key: accept responsibility. That is the turning point in taking complete control of the development of your own personality, of the improvement of your self-concept, and of the raising of your own self-esteem and self-confidence.

Dan

It strikes me that there are products, medical cures, successful marriages, songs, movies, that are essentially stillborn. They are never given birth because of a lack of motivation. There are people that have a certain level of creativity and ability, but they never give birth to it. A lot of times people will say, "I had that idea many years ago." Like the idea of the massaging shower head. I remember someone telling me years ago, "I had that idea." They almost wanted to take credit for the fact that they had the idea.

There are so many great creative projects and works of art within many, many people in our society. Really the only thing that separates out the successful ones is the motivation to get it done.

Brian

Yes. To go back to early childhood experiences, you can grow up with a semiautomatic response to any opportunity. The first response of the person who has had a difficult upbringing—and the most ruinous of all actions that human beings can take—is destructive criticism. Destructive criticism triggers anger and negativity in the recipient. I call it a mental cancer.

When this kind of person has an experience or an opportunity, the very first automatic reaction is "Wouldn't that be great!" and the second reaction is "But I can't, I can't because, because . . ." They trot out all the old reasons. *I don't have enough time. I don't have enough money. I'm not well educated. I'm just too tired at the end of the day.* They go on and on automatically. They stomp out the fire of motivation before it even gets going.

Here are the three major reasons people do not accomplish things. The first is the *comfort zone.* They say, "I can't because I'm so busy doing it this way." The comfort zone is the greatest enemy of success today. People may fight to get into a comfort zone, or they may get into it gradually or unknowingly, but then they fight like terriers to stay there, even when they know it's not a good place to be.

Apple came out with the iPhone in 2006–2007, and it had these incredible new features that had never been in a cellular phone before. The senior executives at both Nokia and Blackberry looked at this and said, "It's just a fad. It's for kids who want to have social media and playback, and exchange words with their friends, take photographs, and share them, and so on." They just ignored it.

Blackberry cut their R&D budget that year by 50%, because, they said, "We don't need to upgrade or improve our phones: we've got 49% of the world business market," and they did. Nokia had 50% of the world's cellular phone market, and they said, "We don't need to change anything. Everybody loves our products. Why wouldn't they? We're the biggest and the best in the world." Five years later, both companies were gone because they could not get out of a comfort zone, They didn't realize that with a new technology like the iPhone, the entire world of communications had changed.

They say that the average person with an iPhone 6 has one billion times the computing power of the first computers put together in 1947—what they called Turing machines, after Alan Turing of England. A person today has a billion times more capacity in his pocket. We can do extraordinary things. If you look at the rapid change, what we'll be able to do in five years with your cell phone is just beyond our imagination.

The comfort zone is a great killer. You have to ask yourself, "Am I holding myself back by refusing to accept that the world is changing?" And the world *is* changing. Eighty percent of all products and services that we're using today will be obsolete and gone from the market within five years and will be replaced with brand-new products, services, people, and companies. Eighty percent of jobs will have changed dramatically.

In America we lose about 3 million jobs a year, and we create about 3.2 million jobs a year, so there's a huge ebb and flow, like the tides coming in and out. Three million jobs are made obsolete by changes in the market, taste, and everything else. Fortunately, because of the dynamism of the American economy, 3.2 million jobs on average are created. Not only are we replacing the jobs that have been made obsolete, but we've added about 200,000 more. That's the way our economy normally grows; that's how we maintain low levels of unemployment.

The second reason people don't accomplish things is *fear of failure*. Fear of failure is characterized by the words, "I can't. I can't. I'd like to do it, but I can't, I can't, because . . ." Successful people turn it around and say, "I can do anything I put my mind to. I could do this. I could do that. That's just a new skill." Their whole idea is, "I can do it." The only question is "How do I do it? Where can I learn how? I'll get a book. I'll talk to somebody. I'll go online." It never occurs to them that they can't do something, and that's a tremendous transformation.

The third major reason people don't accomplish things is that they feel that they don't know how to make the change. They feel ignorant. *Of course I'd like to start a business, but I don't know how.* That's why I put together my early work with Nightingale-Conant. I put together a fabulous program called *How to Start, Build, Manage, or Turn Around Any Business.* It became the best-selling program of its kind on startups and business growth in the world. I'm still being asked to give parts of it all around the world.

People say, "I want to write a book." Eighty-two percent of American adults want to write a book, but they don't know where to start. I put together a program, *How to Write a Book and Get Published.* People take it, and they're just astonished. Within ninety days they've got a book and a publisher, and they'd been dreaming about it for years. The reason people don't take action is that they don't know how.

Those are the three reasons: people become too comfortable; they have a natural fear which comes from destructive criticism in childhood and perhaps early failures; and they're ignorant. They don't know how.

Dan

Great advice. Let's talk about this idea that motivation is really what makes us human and reveals the best of the human capability. We worry about being replaced by computers, but computers are basically stimulus-response: they get an input, and they respond in a certain way. Animals are very much the same way. There are less intelligent animals, but basically, with animals, there is a stimulus, and then there is a response.

Human beings are different. As Stephen Covey pointed out, they encounter a stimulus, then there's a response, but in the middle there's a freedom to choose. Can you talk a little bit about this idea that if we don't make use of motivation, we're not making use of this greatest of human gifts that separates us from computers and animals?

Brian

Actually it takes place in the way that you respond or react. There's a moment where you can think. As your mother told you, stop and think before you act. Stop and think before you speak. Rich people stop and think before they speak. Poor people say whatever is on their mind. You don't have to say everything you're thinking. You don't have to blurt anything out, so you just stop.

I've found that if you're on the verge of saying something and the other person interrupts you, it's God's way of telling you not to speak. Instead of trying to speak over the other person or win the discussion, stop and think. People cause problems by saying things without giving them enough thought.

In fact, the second major reason people fail is that they do things without giving them enough thought. Successful people stop and think. Sometimes they stop and think for a long time. Peter Drucker had a wonderful one-liner: "Fast people decisions are invariably wrong people decisions." He said, "Whenever you have to make a decision with futurity," which means it's going to last for a long time, "take a lot of time to think. Take a day, take a weekend."

There was an excellent book written about decision making a couple of years ago. The writer's major point was this: the more time you can put between the stimulus and the response, the more effective, the better will be the response. The more time you can put between the need to make a decision and making the decision, the better and higher quality the decision will be. That's why they say to sleep on it, or sleep on it over the weekend. If you have to make any kind of a decision that has futurity, one of the smartest things of all is to say, "Let me think about it for a couple of days." If somebody wants to borrow money or sell you something or asks you to give up your time to do something else, you say, "It sounds like a good idea, but let me think about it for a while."

The biggest mistakes I've ever made happened when I responded too quickly without giving it any thought. I found later that I'd made a dreadful mistake. I said, "I could kick myself. Why didn't I just take some time to think about that? Why did I respond in such a knee-jerk way?"

Many years ago I had a mentor who had a great effect on me. He gave me a beautiful old book from the '20s, called *Take Time Out for Mental Digestion*. The book explains how you need seventy-two hours to incorporate a new idea into your thinking. When you have a new idea or opportunity, always take seventy-two hours—that's the basic rule—to think about it and turn it over in your mind. Look at it from several different aspects before you finally make a decision.

In working as a personal advisor to extremely wealthy people, people with hundreds of millions and billions of dollars, I found that they take a lot of time to make decisions. They go through a lot of research. They do a lot of pondering. They talk it over with other intelligent people. They ask for more information. As a result, when they do make the decision, the decision is vastly better than if they had reacted immediately.

Most successful people are more thoughtful than unsuccessful people. It's not that they're smarter, they just take more time and gather more information. They use that middle point in Covey's little model. They're free to choose the time and the response. They use that moment, and they use it very generously.

Drucker used to say that if you're going to hire someone, take a week, take a month, spend some time with them, but go very slowly, especially if you're starting a business or running a fast-growing business. Be very careful, because if you hire the wrong person, the complexities and costs and losses can be tremendous in a small business, as every small-business person has experienced: "If I had given it a little more thought I would have never hired him or her in the first place."

That's how you work. You take the time and sit down and turn off the radio and the music. You turn off the computer and the phone and sit quietly and really think about important decisions. It's one of the greatest discoveries for success.

Dan

Excellent. I like that seventy-two-hour rule you talked about, because that gives you a nice balance between taking the time to think and excessive pondering—overthinking to avoid making a decision. That seems like a good balance for making sure that you are using that time to give the matter full consideration, while still in the end taking a decisive approach without sitting forever in thought.

Brian, sometimes when something new comes up, it can bring a person out of their comfort zone. They have to make a decision, but when they think about it, maybe they come up with excuses to stay the same. How do you use that decision time to think through something while making sure you're challenging yourself rather than using that thinking time to pull yourself back in?

Brian

One question I ask my audience is, "How many people here would like to double their income?" Of course everybody raises their hand. I say, well, "That's good, because you are going to double your income. As an economist I can guarantee that everyone here in this room is going to double their income if they live long enough, because if your income goes up at the average of about 3% per annum using compound interest, you'll double your income in twenty-two years. Is that what you have in mind?" Everybody says, "No, no."

So you want to double your income much faster. All right. Well, here's an interesting discovery. If you increase your income by 25% per year, with compounding, you'll double your income in three years. If you continue to increase your income at 25% per year for ten years, you'll increase your income ten times. There's a formula for increasing your income ten times; we'll talk about it later. It's a matter of specific rituals that you engage in every single day.

I say, "How do you increase your income 25% per year? Well, you increase it 2% per month, or 0.5% a week. If you become more productive 0.05% each week, 2% a month, then the compounding effect will guarantee that you'll double and double again. You'll become one of the highest paid people in our society, completely irrespective of your background, grades, friends, contacts, or the state of the economy. Is that possible?" Everybody says, "Of course it's possible." I say, "Then just take the first step."

Time management is very simple. You should plan every day in advance. You decide on your most important task. You start on that task first, and you complete it before you go on to number two. I've written a book on this; it is the best-selling book on time management in history, 6 million copies sold in forty-two languages. It teaches every single part of time management, but it distills it down to choosing your most important task. Start on that first thing, and stay with it until it's done. If you do that, you'll double your productivity next week, not in three years, and your income will soon catch up with your increased productivity.

People say, "Of course. I could do that." Yes. The way that you succeed is one step at a time. You don't have to transform your life. You ask, how do you get people out of their comfort zone? Warren Bennis did a best-selling book called *Leaders.* They studied ninety-three leaders over a five-year period. These were top people: university presidents, top corporation presidents, the head of a philharmonic orchestra. The researchers even lived in their homes to watch them and talk to them in order to find out how they were different.

One thing was, leaders were always conscious of slipping into a comfort zone. They kept themselves out of the comfort zone by setting such big goals for themselves that it was impossible for them to achieve them at their current level of activity. They would have to move out of their comfort zone to accomplish these huge goals. These "b-hogs"—big, hairy, audacious goals. They all did that.

That's why I say to my audience, "If you'd like to double your income, I'll give you several ways to do it, ways that are used by the most productive people. If you'll do them, you'll dramatically move yourself out of your comfort zone. You'll see results within a week as you begin to apply these techniques." It is results that motivate people.

Daniel Pink wrote a really good book called *Drive: The Surprising Truth about What Motivates Us*. The book was a state-of-the-art analysis of what drives people. The answer was, as you and I have discussed, forward motion, progress, the feeling *I'm getting better in my job. I'm making progress in my career. I am earning more money. I'm achieving more of my goals. I'm doing more of the things that I want to do.* This feeling of forward movement is the greatest motivator of all, and it's totally under the individual's control.

Dan

Outstanding. Is there one final thought that you want to leave with people on why motivation is so important to people's success?

Brian

I always say that motivation requires a motive. We'll talk about this later. One of the most important reasons why people are not motivated is they have no motive. They have no *why*. They have no goal. They have no something great that they want to accomplish. If that happens, if they come across something that really excites them, suddenly they're instantly motivated. They're up out of bed early in the morning. They're in it all day long. They're busy in the evening. They become impatient with small talk, because now they've got a motive. Now they've got something big that they want to accomplish.

One best-selling book is called *Start with Why* by Simon Sinek. Why are you doing what you're doing? Why do you get up in the morning? What are your values? Once you have that, you say, "I want to earn more money so that I can create a better life for my family, so I can create opportunities for my children, so I can take them places and do things for them." That's what gets you out of bed in the morning. But each person is responsible for determining their motive, their *why*, their what it is they want to accomplish, and of course what they will do when they've accomplished it. That's what motivates people.

TWO

The Myths of Motivation and the Truths That Will Set You Free

Dan

Brian, here I want to have you highlight some of the most commonly believed myths about what it takes to be motivated. A lot of people want the outcome that you've talked about: to be motivated, to have something that really gets them up in the morning and drives them. And yet that kind of dream often doesn't become reality, because a lot of people engage in myths.

Myth number one is the myth that motivation can be supplied by outside forces, such as a motivational speaker, an improving economy, a raise, or a promotion—something like that. Why is that a myth, and what is the truth?

Brian

As you say, motivation comes from within and requires a motive. I've been a motivational speaker for years. I believe there are two types of motivation. There is *false motivation* and there is *true motivation*. False motivation is where you are told a lot of funny stories about how you can do anything and so on. There are some very successful people who teach this. It's a feel-good type of motivation, like going to a great movie or a rock concert, but it has no lasting value. People forget 80% or 90% of what they heard, even though they felt good when they were listening to it.

I've always focused on true motivation. True motivation, in my estimation, comes from an enhanced feeling of competence. The speaker gives you specific things that you can do to help you to achieve your goals faster and have a better life immediately. That's what motivates people, because when they learn new skills or new ideas, they say, "I can do that," whether we're teaching sales skills or personal development, time management, or goal setting skills, or teaching how to build a successful business. People think, "I can do that. That's not complicated. That's very practical, and I can see the result I can get."

Here's a wonderful thing about motivation: people are not motivated unless they can create a mental picture, an exciting visual picture of themselves actually doing what they're either reading or hearing about from a speaker. They can actually see themselves saying, "I can do that. I can get up a little bit earlier." Rich people get up before 6 a.m. Poor people get up at 7 a.m. or later—a very simple thing. Start to change your habits, including when you rise. We'll talk about this later with regard to the rituals of successful people and how to make them habits.

I told you about my mentor who gave me that book, *Take Time Out for Mental Digestion*. He made a habit of getting up before 6 a.m. every morning. His company had fifty-two branches and 10,000 employees, and he ran the manufacturing operation in the city. He'd started off working at the lowest level job, in the mail room in a large company, and worked himself up.

He said to me, "I always get up before 6 a.m. If I go to bed late, I still force myself to get up before 6 a.m., but that teaches me a good lesson not to go to bed late the second night in a row." In other words, if you set a very simple discipline about when you're going to get up, the whole rest of your life iterates almost like an Excel program. It changes everything that happens for the rest of the day.

Your motivation comes from inside yourself, and you can create that motivation. And the way you create that motivation is by having something to get yourself out of bed for in the morning.

Dan

Excellent. **Myth number two** is one that in some ways is being fostered these days by neuroscience. There's been some suggestion by neuroscience that there are people who are hard-wired toward an optimistic outlook, and others that aren't. Motivation, or what some people might call optimism, is just something you're born with: there are people who are wired to be positive and motivated and those that aren't.

Do you feel that this is a myth? And for people who feel that they haven't gotten that hard wiring, how can they develop it?

Brian

It goes back to our discussion of self-concept. In the early formative experiences of the individual, were they constantly encouraged and praised and approved of and made to feel valuable, important, and smart? In that case, they're going to grow up to be highly motivated and positive about themselves and their potential.

Now here's something that I learned, and it has to do with self-esteem lying at the root of your self-concept. Your self-concept is made up of three parts. The first part is called your *self-ideal*. Your self-ideal is the person that you would ideally like to be. It's your fantasy person—in terms of health and wealth and position and influence and marriage and everything else. This ideal is either clear, as it is in the minds of successful people, or it's unclear. Unsuccessful people are vague and unclear about where they would like to be in the future.

So one question I ask is, if you could wave a magic wand and make your life perfect three years from now, what would it look like, and how would it be different from today? And I help people take the time to write it down: how much they would be earning, what kind of home they would live in, what kind of relationship status or marriage they would have, what level of health and fitness they would have, how much money they'd have in the bank.

As people start to think about that and become clear about it, motivation takes place automatically. So the second part of a self-concept, like the second wedge in a pie, is your *self-image*. The self-image is how you see yourself, and it regulates your performance on a moment to moment basis. We always perform on the outside consistently with the picture we have on the inside. There's a saying, *the person you see is the person you'll be*. Your self-image is also made up of three parts. It's the way you see yourself, the way others see you, and the way you think others see you.

If you think other people see you as an excellent person, when you go to a party or you associate with them, you'll be happy and they'll be happy. That's why, whenever you're with your friends or your family, and they all know you and like you and love you and respect you, you're happy all the time. You don't have any problems with public speaking here. You speak extemporaneously and you talk and you laugh, because they are reinforcing your self-image as a likeable, attractive, intelligent person. But if we have the wrong idea of how people see us, if we think that they see us in a negative way, it'll affect our performance.

And so there's the way people see you and the way you think they see you. When a parent is warm and friendly and loving and treats their child as if they're wonderful, the child's self-image is *I'm a wonderful person. I'm a good person. I'm a great person. I'm a happy person. I'm a successful person.*

I was just at my grown son's home. They know all this stuff, and they practice it on their two little girls. The youngest is one year old and the older one is three. These kids laugh all the time. It's the true measure of the health of personalities: how much people laugh and how much they laugh together.

Now there's a gap between your *self-image*, the way you see yourself now, and your *self-ideal*, the way you would like to be in the future, and this gap determines the quality of your personality. If you feel there's a huge gap between where you are now and where you could be, it demotivates you. You lose heart.

That's why people say, "I want to be a millionaire." OK, let's write it down, make a plan, set a schedule. "I want to be a millionaire within a year." How much money do you have now? "I'm broke." What sort of work do you do? "I'm unemployed." How much money do you have in the bank? "None, I'm deeply in debt."

Setting a goal to be a millionaire, the ideal, contrasted with where you are today, will simply demotivate you. It will not inspire you. You'll take a couple of stabs at it and give up and then you'll tell yourself that it wasn't meant to be anyway.

The third wedge of the pie is *self-esteem*. Your self-esteem is best defined as how much you like yourself, how much your love yourself, how much you value and appreciate yourself as a truly important and worthwhile person. This is the reactor core, this is the heartbeat. This is the critical determinant of the quality of your personality. It determines your self-image. As you move from your image of where you are more and more toward your ideal of where you want to be, your self-esteem goes up. You like yourself more, you feel good about yourself, and you feel happy and you laugh out loud. You feel exuberant.

There's nothing to seize like success. It's not the material rewards. It's the inner joy that you receive. The way that you raise your self-esteem is you simply repeat *I like myself. I like myself. I like myself.*

I saw a video just the other day by this young guy, who's extraordinarily successful, and when he heard that the speaker was a good friend of mine, he said, "I want to send him a video." So he sat him down and for seven minutes he just fired into the video about how his life had sucked. He was in sales. He was selling cellular telephones in a shopping center. He would talk to fifty people, and they'd all tell him to go away, forget about it, get out of here. He was in such despair, and then he went out and got one of my books called *The Psychology of Selling,* and he read it. It says that how you feel on the inside is going to determine how successful you are on the outside.

The next day when he went to work, he sat in the car and said, "I like myself. I like myself. I like myself." People were looking at him because he was talking to himself. He went into the shopping center. A person he talked to said no, but he said, "Wait a minute. This is really a good choice. This can revolutionize your life."

He became on fire, because he had cranked up his self-esteem and his self-confidence. The person said, "Really? Tell me more about it." and he made his first sale after several days of talking to people. Then he made his second sale and his third sale. Pretty soon he was blowing the record book. He became a supervisor, and then he became a manager. Then he was hired by a bigger company and he said, "Saying 'I like myself, I like myself, I like myself' transformed my life completely."

The two most powerful pillars of the mental temple are *I like myself* and *I am responsible. I like myself. I am responsible*. The more you like yourself, the more responsibility you accept. The more responsibility you accept, the more powerful you feel, and the more you like yourself. There's a direct relationship between how much you like yourself and how positive you are. There's a direct relationship between how much responsibility you accept, how much you feel in control of your own life, and how happy you are overall. Each one reinforces the other.

Dan

Brian, we're in the midst of a presidential election. This idea of I *am responsible* is so powerful, and yet you see so many people who hold politicians responsible for their future. They bank their future on the kind of job they'll get, or the wages they're going to be paid, on the promise of some politician.

Talk about that dynamic and show us how no matter what side of the spectrum people are on, turning over responsibility to a politician is only going to set yourself up for more frustration and failure.

Brian

Right. I wrote a book a few years ago called *Something for Nothing*. Based on forty years of psychological and political research, it explained that the lowest common denominator of people is that they want something for free. They want free stuff. They want free money. They want things that they have not earned and do not deserve.

Now politics is essentially the business of getting votes, and just as in a customer market, companies emerge to provide the product that they want. The great majority of people want to get more than they put in. They want to get out more. They want to have free things. They want to have things that are discounted and so on.

So in America today 47% of the population are taking out more than they're putting in, and they like that. Free money makes people crazy. The threat of taking away free money makes people go insane. They get into the streets and they riot and they scream and they break windows when you say we're going to start to cut back on the free money. They can get a mob out there with thousands of people screaming.

Now the reason is that if there is a customer base for a particular philosophy, such as free money, politicians will emerge to represent those people. They will tell these people, "You deserve this free money," and they will give 100 reasons for it.

There's an interesting way of structuring a talk. It's called "the villain, the victim, and the hero." Steve Jobs used this method, and other speakers use it as well. It's a very simple way of designing a talk. First of all, you talk about the villain. The villain is them successful people, them millionaires and billionaires that got all this money. They're the reason you are not earning more money, getting more money, enjoying more programs, living in a bigger house.

You're the victim, so they say, "Here's the victim, and I'm the hero. I will save you from the villain. All I need is your support. Just support me, and I'll protect you from the villain, and I'll make sure that you get as much free money as possible."

In every society there are two types of people. There are the people who believe in hard work and opportunity and wealth creation. It's building businesses by producing products and services that people want and need and are willing to pay for. Wealthy people always think in terms of creating wealth. They always think in terms of earning more money by satisfying more customers. This has been the foundation of the American republic for more than 200 years.

There are also a lot of other people who don't understand the connection between serving people and earning a lot of money, so they say, "I should be given more money." Why? "Because I live in this country. Lots of people in this country are richer than me, and I should get my fair share." There are always politicians who will arise to say, "Let me be your hero. Vote for me and I'll get you free money and free stuff." That argument is very attractive to people. They know that it's not right and they know that it's not possible to get money you don't deserve. It's a form of theft. They know that it's wrong, but they're too weak, so they vote for the party that says, "Vote for me and I'll give you everything free."

Where is it going to come from? From the millionaires and billionaires. The fact is if you taxed 100% of the income of the wealthiest Americans away, you could run the federal government for forty-six days. Then the country would be bankrupt for the next twenty years, and there would be no jobs for anyone.

So this idea of taxing the millionaires and billionaires means ultimately we'll have to tax anybody who has a job. That's why they say the average income hasn't gone up for so many years. The average income has gone up, but the taxes and all the charges have gone up as well, so now it takes two people to work to get to take home what one working person was making twenty years ago, because the taxes are so high.

Today, if a wife decides to go to work, her taxes will be 50% or more, so for every dollar she earns because of the combined income of her husband and herself, they'll take $0.50 of that additional dollar. And then there'll be all kinds of charges and social charges and so on. What will be done with this money? It'll be used to buy more votes, so that they can get more power, so that they can do this again and again, and they just keep the game going.

That's the problem today. There are people who want to create a society in America where there's opportunity and self-reliance and hard work, and where you could start and build businesses and you can achieve wonderful things through your own tenacity and purpose and innovation. There are others who would prefer to just have it given to them. The politicians represent one constituency or the other.

Dan

So you're saying that regardless of the political environment, almost regardless of the economy, whether we're in recession or whether we're in boom times, by employing the ideas you're talking about around motivation and goal orientation, you can essentially exempt yourself from the people who worry about these conditions.

Brian

Don't go out and *have* a good day, go out and *make it* a good day. We have more opportunities surrounding us today, because there are more products and services being invented and more customer wants and needs being unsatisfied, so there's always something that somebody can do in order to go out there and take advantage of our market situation. But it requires ambition. It requires hard work. It requires persistence and tenacity and bouncing back over and over again, and the great majority of people just don't want to do that. Maybe it's because of early childhood experiences; they just don't have the grit.

The New York Times did a study on this and now several books have been written. It basically says that all of the studies on psychology come down to the quality of grit. This person has grit, determination, tenacity, they will not be stopped. They will start and they will try something, and they'll try something else, and they'll try something else.

One of my favorite stories is about Mike Todd, who was a great impresario and producer in New York. He was married to Elizabeth Taylor. He put up the money to sponsor plays. Sometimes they worked, sometimes they didn't. One day he put all of his money behind this play and he lost it all, and the announcement was "Mike Todd is broke."

A reporter came and asked, "Mr. Todd, what is it like to be poor?" He said, "Excuse me, young man, I'm not poor; I'm only broke. Poor is a state of mind; broke is a temporary condition, and I will be back." And he was. His next show was a great success, and he was back being a multimillionaire and a member of high society.

This is one of the greatest observations: broke is a temporary condition; poor is a state of mind. If you're poor, you only think of how you can get money from other people. How can I get more money than I deserve? How can I live with my situation? And then you always support people who say, "Support me and I'll get you some free money and some free stuff."

It's not so much that this is wrong financially or politically, although it is. It's that free money destroys the soul of the recipient. Earned money, earned success, is the foundation principle for self-esteem, self-reliance, self-responsibility, happiness, joy, energy. When you earn your success, you feel great.

They used to say that rich people aren't happy. I've studied the rich, and I can tell you the rich are very happy, because they have started with nothing; 90% of all successful Americans started with nothing, and they have achieved something worthwhile through ten, twenty, thirty years of hard work. Now they have it—a nice home and a nice car and a great life and everything else.

People say they were just lucky. Then you look at their backgrounds. They started off like me, washing dishes. They started off working on a ship to get here. They lived in slums for weeks and months and years while they were working their way up.

Andrew Grove, who recently died, was the president of Intel— one of the great entrepreneurs in American history. His name was originally András Gróf, and he was from Hungary. When the Russians overran Hungary in 1956, he fled to New York. He learned English, and he went to school and got an engineering degree. Then he went out west and got a business degree, and then he started at the bottom of a business in San Francisco. Before it was over, he was the president of Intel, the biggest microchip and computer chip manufacturer in the world. If you ever listen to him or read anything he wrote, you will see that he was a great man. He arrived here with nothing, a sixteen-year-old fleeing the revolution. People say, "He sure was lucky." Behind every lucky person there's a long history of hard work and countless failures.

I was talking to somebody recently who was saying this—successful people are just lucky. They just stumbled into it. They just hit it. I said to him, "You're an intelligent guy. Did you know that successful people fail five and ten times more often than failures do?" And he blew up at me. He said, "That's not true. Successful people just fell in the jam. They just stumbled into something and it turned out to be the right thing." I said, "No, statistically speaking, successful people fail over and over and over again vastly more than the average person."

They had a radio interview with four self-made millionaires a few years ago. They asked them just prior to the break, "How many different businesses have you been in before you got into the one where you made a million dollars?" During the break they calculated it out. They came back, and it was an average of seventeen businesses. They had failed, or semi-failed, in sixteen businesses. It was the seventeenth one, on average, that made them rich. So they asked, "Did you actually fail in the first sixteen businesses?" and all four of them said, "No, those are the most important learning experiences. Without those failures, we would have never been successful in the business we're in today."

Dan

That's incredible. That leads right into **myth number three**, Brian, which is that motivation can only arise out of positive events or circumstances. Certainly it helps when you're surrounded by a supportive community and so forth and have positive inputs. But as you've said—as with Andy Grove fleeing the revolution, starting out in difficult circumstances—the choice to motivate oneself can arise both from positive and negative emotions or circumstances.

There is also this concept in neurolinguistic programming, NLP, which says that some people are motivated by moving towards a positive outcome, but other people are motivated by moving away from a negative outcome, and that in many ways is as much of fuel. Talk about how you can use either the positive or the negative to motivate yourself.

Brian

To start with the negative, it's a basic foundation principle in psychology that we always strive to achieve as adults what we felt we were most deprived of as children. If we felt we were deprived of money, we'll often aspire to get money, or will be driven to it. If we felt that we were deprived of love and support, we will strive to get love and support from a member of the opposite sex. If we felt that we were ignored or useless in school, we'll strive for respect from other people, or we'll strive to do something.

Most of the actors in Hollywood are driven by this feeling of being important because when they were young, they were made to feel unimportant and useless. So they have this drive. They started to get the taste of show biz, where people clap and applaud and smile and shake their hands and tell them what a great job they did. It becomes a drug.

Henry Ford once said that power is the ultimate aphrodisiac, because when you have lots of power, you feel incredible about yourself. You feel powerful. People come to you. They shake your hand, they ask for your autograph, and they listen to you when you speak. That's coming from the negative, and it's very common.

I was talking with three wealthy businesspeople the other day, and I said, "When did you get your first job?" Ten or eleven was when they got their first jobs. When I was ten, my parents told me, "We just don't have the money to buy you clothes for school, so you're going to have to earn it yourself." This was in the summertime. And I said, "OK" and got a garden hoe. I went out knocking on doors and asking people if they had any weeds to hoe. I finally found this very nice woman who said, "Come and take a look at this." Her whole backyard was overgrown. She said, "Can you hoe those weeds?" I said, "Absolutely." "How much do you charge?" "Twenty-five cents an hour." She said, "OK."

And I hoed those weeds. I think it took me two weeks to hoe down that whole yard and rake up that grass and put it into piles and into wheelbarrows and drag it away. That was my money to buy my clothes for the fall. From that day onward, I never took a penny from my parents. I got up and delivered newspapers at 4:00 and 5:00 a.m., as did a couple of my rich friends.

At the age of fourteen Warren Buffett didn't have that much money. He got up at 4:00 every morning to deliver newspapers, and he saved the money from his newspaper route. He got one penny profit for every paper he delivered, and he kept the money because his parents were paying for his food. He delivered 200,000 newspapers over a period of three or four years. He saved $2000. That was a starting point for his investments.

He invested $2000 in 1962. Today he's got $350 billion under management. Last year his profits were $25 billion. He started with that one penny from delivering each newspaper, saved up carefully, getting up at 4:00 in the morning six or seven days a week. People say he's lucky; he's one of the richest men in the world. Yes, and look where he started. That's moving away from the negative.

The positive is equally motivational. It's when it occurs to people that they can be vastly more than they are. This is one of the influences that Maslow had on me when I read that first book. It said you have enormous potential that you can get out of yourself. And so I began spending thousands of hours studying while everybody was out socializing and going to bars and drinking. I'd sit at home hour after hour reading all about success, and that's when I found the importance of eliminating negative emotions. If you eliminate negative emotions, they're automatically replaced by positive emotions, and one of the positive emotions is goals. You start to think about goals. What do I really want to do with my life?

This great question, by the way, has three parts. You ask this question: *what do you really want to do with your life?* And pause, and let people think about it. Then you ask it again: *what do you really, really want to do with your life?* Then you pause and you ask it one more time: *what do you really, really, really want to do with your life?* If you had no restrictions, if you could accomplish anything in the world, if you had all the knowledge and skill and talent and ability that you would ever need, what would you really want to do with your life? If you can determine that, and it's clear to you, and you can see a picture of what it would look like, you're automatically motivated.

It lights up all the afterburners within your psyche. You wake up in the morning, and you're wired to move toward that goal, but you've got to see it clearly. You have to know what it is. You have to know exactly what you want, what you would want to accomplish if you had no limitations at all. That's what motivates you in a positive way.

Dan

Excellent. **Myth number four** is a more subtle one. It says that motivation is a condition of the mind that, once achieved, remains with you for a lifetime. You've been talking about having a goal that we're passionate about and how if people can set that goal and get their mind set on track, their lives will change forever from there. I even heard one motivational speaker say, "Once the lights were turned on for me, they've never turned off."

That's what a lot of people's hopes and dreams are. But often the truth is that motivation is a condition of the mind that must be renewed or restored on a daily basis. Even someone who's been very successful like yourself, Brian—if you don't continually renew and restore, sharpen that saw, even success can start to feel mundane or not fresh anymore. You lose the get-up-and-go that you had once.

Brian

Lloyd Conant was a great man, founder of Nightingale-Conant Corporation. He once told me about a philosophy he had. You have a template for success in your subconscious mind. It's almost like a framework that fills in like concrete. Every successful person has achieved one great goal, and as a result, they have a template for success. Nothing will ever satisfy them more than the achievement of another goal that's even bigger, so all success begins with achieving one big goal.

If you take the 80/20 rule, you'll find that the 20% of people who earn 80% of the money have, sometime in their lives, started and completed a major goal. It may be as simple as graduating from a university or winning a race. It may be climbing a mountain. It may be writing a book or a poem. It may be becoming the president of a society, but they've accomplished *something*. It's called *learned success* or *earned achievement*. They've accomplished something that they had to work hard for, that they could have lost by giving up, but they pushed through.

Once they've done that, because of the joy they get, the endorphins are released. The fireworks go off in their brain. Sometimes they'll look back decades later and say, "That was the great moment of my life." I've spoken to people just in the last couple of weeks who can look back to their first great success. It was a high point in their lives.

From then on you're actually programmed, almost like a computer, to achieve another success that's even greater. You'll wake up every morning and all you're going to think of is, what is going to be my next success? What is it going to be? You're looking forward. You read and you go to seminars and workshops. You're constantly learning new things, looking for your next big success.

So my advice is to pick one goal that's really important to you. Then put your whole heart into achieving it, no matter how long it takes, because once you do that, you'll become a different person and a better person for the rest of your life.

Dan

When I was at college at Notre Dame, I had a friend whose whole objective in life had been to get into Notre Dame. That was his big thing. He struggled in high school, so he went to a community college, got straight A's for two years, and then got into Notre Dame. But the irony was that about two months before graduation, his grades collapsed, because Notre Dame to him was the ultimate. This was where he wanted to be, and the idea of graduating and leaving depressed him. He never set that next goal that you're talking about.

You see some people who always look back to when they were captain of the football team in high school. They had one success, but they never had the next one. The key is setting that first goal, but then be prepared for the next one and then the next one. It's a continual process.

Brian

Yes, they did a study of two teams that played in the Super Bowl. Both teams of course had won their leagues and won their divisions. One team beat the other 45–8 or something like that—one of those upset victories.

They interviewed the players on the teams afterwards What you visualize has a tremendous effect on your motivation. Throughout the season, one team had visualized winning every game, getting into the Super Bowl, running onto the field at the Super Bowl, with the crowds cheering, hundreds of thousands of people, and the music. They visualized this in their locker room, and they talked about it over and over again.

The other team was visualizing running *off* the field in the Super Bowl with the trophy. So the one team may have accomplished their goal when they ran onto the field. That was it; they fell apart on the field because they had no further vision or goal.

The other team visualized themselves winning this game and running off as champions.

Every goal should lead to a higher goal, and you should already have determined your next goal when you move toward completion of this goal, so each goal motivates you even further, like ranges of mountains beyond ranges of mountains. Each time you cross a mountain, you see higher and higher mountains.

Dan

Myth number five is that motivation alone is sufficient to achieve any goal that you set your mind upon. Some people get lost in this idea—that if I just pump myself up enough, if I'm just motivated, that I'll achieve my goal. But there are other key elements in there that are critically important.

You've talked about this. Motivation is a bridge between thought or ideas and action. All three must be present for achieving a goal. You need to have the idea and the motivation to bridge it, and then take the action.

Brian

People often fall prey to two mistakes in thinking. *Fortune* magazine did a study on this some years ago. The first thinking mistake is *because I want to, I can*. A lot of people are misled by motivational speakers and books.

A perfect example would be *The Secret* by Rhonda Byrne. The law of attraction goes back 4000 years. I've been teaching it for thirty-five years, and I know a lot about the subject.

Rhonda Byrne taught that if you could think happy thoughts and visualize happy pictures and roll your eyes and so on, all good things would come to you, but nowhere in the book does the word *work* appear. People love the book because they love the idea of being successful without having to work, and it became a best seller.

The idea was if I want to, I can. If I want to—that's all that's necessary. I just have to have intense burning desire, but no, that is just the start. Looking at the map and determining what your destination is and then driving out and starting to move towards your destination—that's the beginning.

The second thinking error is *because I have to, I can.* Because I have to, I have to. I've got to earn this money. I've got achieve this goal. What you want to do, what you *have to* do has no relationship to what you *can* do. One of my favorite lines says, "Pray and then move your feet." It means be really clear about your goal, write it down, and then move your feet.

So one thing we'll teach later is the importance of making a detailed plan, a checklist for the accomplishment of a goal. Any big goal is going to have twenty or thirty or forty steps, so you break it down into these steps. Then you take one step at a time. It's like climbing a long staircase: you just plod one step at a time. Each day you get up and you work on one of those steps, and you do them in sequence.

At the beginning there's very little motivation, because progress seems to be very slow, but as you start to move, there's a law called *the law of accelerating acceleration.* As you start to move towards your goal, you create a force field in the universe that starts to attract your goal toward you. Imagine the roundness of the globe. You start to move towards your goal way over on this side of the globe. The goal starts to move toward you too, but you can't see it, because it's on the other side of the globe. It's out of your sight, but as you move toward it, it starts to move toward you.

Like attracts like; bodies in motion will attract each other. As things start moving toward each other, they'll start to move faster and faster. It's the law of physics that Sir Isaac Newton discovered.

Here's a discovery: 80% of your goal will be achieved in the last 20% of the time that you work on your goal. Many people work for a long time and don't see a lot of progress, yet they hang in there and they hang in there, and then suddenly everything starts to work for them. They start to move faster and faster, and they achieve the goal, always in a way that's remarkably different from what they'd initially expected. But the thing is to start by taking one step at a time.

Earl Nightingale used to say that happiness is the progressive realization of a worthy ideal or goal. The step-by-step moving towards something that's important to you gives you a continuous feedback of motivation, a continuous source of energy. It makes you smarter and makes you more creative, just this act of forward motion.

There's another principle that again comes from Sir Isaac Newton. He called it *inertia*: a body in motion tends to remain in motion unless acted upon by an outside force. By the outside force, he meant something like gravity: if you threw a ball, the ball would go through the air, then gravity would start to pull it down to the earth. But if the ball was in open space, where there is no gravity, you could throw it, and it would keep moving to infinity.

There is also *the momentum principle of success.* It says that when you start moving toward your goal, progress will seem very slow at the beginning. This is where most people quit. That's why they say if you want to lose a lot of weight, don't weigh yourself for the first two weeks of your diet and exercise regimen, because you won't see any progress. The progress is starting to take place below the surface, but you won't see it, so wait two weeks. You may find that you may have dropped five pounds. Then you start to become more confident. *This is working. I can do this. This is worthwhile.*

And then somebody asks, "Have you lost weight?" That's considered to be the best single compliment in America, by the way—to ask a person if they've lost weight. They always look at themselves and say, "I don't know." But it's a flattering comment. People love it, especially people who need to hear it.

As you begin to move toward your goal, you get more and more motivation. Almost everything depends upon your belief. If you absolutely believe that you're going to achieve this goal sooner or later, if you just keep working at it, nothing will stop you. Each time you take a step toward the goal, your belief grows. It grows from zero belief or even a negative belief.

In one psychology study, you start off with disbelief. You say, *I want to become wealthy*, but you don't believe it. *But I can become wealthy by setting goals. I'm going to start to work every day.* As we keep doing things and taking steps, the disbelief begins to get smaller and smaller and smaller until you reach a psychologically neutral point.

At this point you neither believe nor disbelieve; you just keep on acting, and then something happens, and your belief goes like a flash. You start to believe a little bit more, and then you keep doing more things, and then your belief starts to grow and grow.

Pretty soon you get to the point where your belief is so big that you become absolutely unstoppable. Nothing can stop you from achieving this goal, because you absolutely 100% believe that it's attainable for you, and that becomes true.

Dan

Excellent, Brian. What final thought do you want to leave with people about myths and misconceptions about motivation? What truth should they focus on to motivate themselves?

Brian

Og Mandino once told me, "Brian, there are no secrets of success. There are merely timeless truths that have been learned and repeated over and over again throughout the centuries." If you go back and read some of the smartest thinkers in antiquity, like Cicero and Plutarch, you'll find that they teach the same principles. You decide very clearly on your objective. Plan your attack, put your plan into action, take action immediately, and just keep working away until you achieve it. It's not a secret. It's been proven over and over by millions of people who are successful today, so anybody can do it.

You have within you more potential than you could ever use, but the potential is only released when you focus it on something that you really want. Nick at Nightingale-Conant used to say that each person has a success mechanism and a failure mechanism. The failure mechanism goes off automatically, which is the reason why 80% of the population is mediocre, stuck in the middle, and worried about money all the time.

The success mechanism has to be triggered, and it's triggered by a goal. If you set a goal, the success mechanism actually becomes the default and causes the failure mechanism to cut off. You can actually shut off your failure mechanism by overriding it with a goal. As long as you're working on the goal, the failure mechanism never comes on again.

THREE

The Power of Beliefs: Turning On Your Action Mechanism

Dan

Brian, I really want to drive home the importance of belief systems, not only in motivating oneself, but in actually getting oneself motivated to take action consistently, without sabotaging oneself for other psychological reasons. In short, it's important to have a simple belief system that supports a person in achievement. I know this has been a huge area that you've discussed throughout your career in many of your books and audio programs. Can you begin by discussing how beliefs are the underlying, often subconscious, triggers that can either support or sabotage your attempts to motivate yourself?

Brian

Yes. This is a wonderful subject. I began studying it forty years ago, and I was staggered by the impact that a person's beliefs have. We talked about your self-concept. Your self-concept is the master program of your mental computer. Everything that you do on the outside is a result of what's been programmed onto your subconscious computer.

Your beliefs are the primary motivators and drivers of motivation because, as Anaïs Nin once said, "You do not believe what you see; you see what you already believe." You go through the world looking through a screen of beliefs, like a lattice that holds up flowers. This screen of beliefs enables you to see some things and not see other things. It causes you to be blinkered, like a horse. You have a narrow view of things, and you can't see anything that's outside these beliefs.

The interesting thing is that all beliefs are learned. Your beliefs about yourself, which determine everything that you think, feel, or do are actually learned from early childhood. Some people are taught positive beliefs. Some people are taught negative beliefs.

Here's an example. There are many people who have very strong beliefs about their religion all over the world. Some people are fanatics, obsessed with their religion. But when those people were born, they knew nothing about their religion at all. Everything they know, think, believe, even will die for today was taught to them over the years, sometimes accidentally, sometimes deliberately.

So the starting point of changing your life is to change your beliefs, because your beliefs determine everything. Now here's a great tragedy: many people have beliefs that are simply not true, and a belief can be accidentally picked up by reading your horoscope or by having someone tell you something and you say, "Well, that makes a lot of sense."

Many years ago, I got bronchitis at Christmastime, the middle of December. Bronchitis tires you out. It's a bad form of a cold, so

I babied myself. I was a bachelor, and I sat around. It was over Christmastime, so I wasn't working, and it went away.

The next year I got it again around Christmastime, and again I had to sit and baby myself for a week. I was convinced that if you have it once, you have it at the same time every year. It was a false belief, but the belief was so strong that right in the middle of December, I would start to have bronchitis. I'd actually make myself sick with a negative belief.

Then I was talking to a friend of mine who was a nurse. I said, "You know, I have bronchitis. I have it every year around Christmastime." She said, "That's absolute nonsense." "Well, somebody had told me that if you have it, you'll have it every year at the same time. It's sort of programmed into your genes." And she said, "That's absolute nonsense. There's no medical foundation for that at all." I said, "Really?" She said, "Absolutely." And I never had bronchitis again for the rest of my life.

Dan

That's incredible. So someone can have a particular belief about themselves and their ability that is so strong that, even if they set a goal and feel they're motivated to achieve that goal, they may find themselves coming short again and again. Do they need to scratch beneath the surface and see the underlying belief that is causing them to come up short?

Brian

The most hindering beliefs are self-limiting beliefs. You're limited in intelligence, because you didn't get great grades. You're limited in ability, because you did not perform at an excellent level. You're limited in creativity, because you haven't come up with any good ideas. You're limited in athletic ability, artistic ability, and so on. It can come from just a casual remark from one of your parents.

My father did not understand any of this. He said, "Brian is completely tone-deaf. He has no ability to listen to or appreciate music." I wanted to get a guitar and play, but he told me I was tone-deaf, and I believed him. I believed him for years, then suddenly I realized, "I may not be a Carnegie Hall musician, but I'm not tone-deaf. I enjoy music." One casual negative remark from someone who you think should know what they're talking about can set you off for life.

Let me give you a positive example. When my son David was growing up, he would try things, and he would be unsuccessful, as kids are at eight, nine, and ten years old. He would say, "Dad, I don't think I can do this. I'm afraid to fail." I said, "David, I'm your father, and I know something about you. I know that you're not afraid of anything. You're not afraid of anything." And he said, "Oh, yes. I'm afraid of a lot of things, at sports and school." I said, "No, you're not afraid of anything. You may think you are. But, I'm your father and I know better. I know that you're not afraid of anything." Then I made a game of it.

Barbara and I would be driving along, and David would be sitting alone or with one of the other kids in the back seat, and I would say, "You know, Barbara, there's one thing I'm really happy about. Our son David is not afraid of anything." I would repeat that, and I called him Dave the Brave. I would say, "How's Dave the Brave today?" And I called him Le Brave, Dave Le Brave, in French. And I would joke around with him.

I just kept repeating this, and then one day I listened to him. He was ten or eleven years old. He was saying to one of his friends, "I know one thing about myself is I'm not afraid of anything." I thought, "Ah, it worked. It worked. I programmed him with repetitious messages, positive single messages." Today David is starting a new business. He's been in three or four different activities. He learned how to sell by knocking on doors. He's in residential real estate. He is not afraid of anything.

Dan

I love that story. So if a person has a set of beliefs that they feel are keeping them from staying motivated, and if these beliefs took a lifetime to get in there from people's comments and upbringing, how long should it take for somebody to effect a new, more positive belief system that can support them toward their goals? What process should they follow?

Brian

The starting point is to challenge your self-limiting beliefs and ask yourself, "In what area do I feel limited in some way?" I started off with no education, no money, no schooling, no anything else. So I had a lot of self-limiting beliefs. Then I began to think that they're not true. It was a real shock. Somebody will tell you something that you believed all your life, like my story about the bronchitis, and it's not true, and when you find that it's not true, suddenly, holy smokes.

I'll give you a great example that I read about very early. It was about a guy who became very successful. He remembered growing up in a working-class family. His father was a factory worker, and his father repeated at the dinner table over and over again, "The Wilsons have always been working people. We've always been laborers. We'll always be laborers. When you kids grow up, you'll be laborers as well. You'll be working for factories in that laboring job, because we have always been laborers, generation after generation."

So when the guy left school, he went out and got a laboring job. One day, about a year or two later, he was nineteen or twenty years old. He was digging a ditch next to the highway, and the traffic was slowed down. A car came along, and there was one of the guys from his high school, who was no smarter than he was, but he was driving a nice car. He was obviously well dressed.

The first guy said, "Glen, how are you doing?" Glen said, "I'm doing great. I got into sales. I got into life insurance. I'm making great money, just bought a new house. I'm getting married in a year."

The traffic moved on, and away he went. The first guy sat there and realized—suddenly, like a flash—he had bought his father's beliefs that he was only suited to be a laborer.

Then he saw somebody who was no smarter than he, no better than he, who had a great life. He got up, threw the shovel in the ditch, and quit. He went out and he got a job in sales, and six years later he was a millionaire and he had his own business. He remembered that turning point: he was working away in the ditch, and somebody came along, and suddenly he realized, "I have been sold a false belief that I'm going to be a laborer all my life."

The reason I use that story is that we all have false beliefs. We all have beliefs that hold us back. They act like brakes on our potential. A good friend of mine, who's a psychologist and a teacher, wrote a book called *Release Your Brakes,* and it's one of the great expressions. *Release Your Brakes.* What are the brakes that are holding you back?

Which is why I say, "How would you like to earn twice as much or five times as much or ten times as much? You're all capable of it. And how do we know that's true?" I will say. "Because there are lots of people around you in the same room selling your same product in this market but who are earning five and ten times as much as you, and they're no smarter than you. Actually some of them are dumber and less educated than you. They say nothing will make you angrier than to find somebody who's dumber than you who's earning more money than you are," and they all laugh, and it's true. These people believe they can do it.

There's an old thing about courage. It ain't bragging if you've done it. So one way you can overcome negative beliefs is you think about the opposite. You say, "I can't earn much more money than I'm earning today. I'm always in debt." Say, "No, I can earn all the money that I want simply by continually upgrading my skills and applying myself very diligently, using my time well and working hard. I can earn the same kind of money that other people do doing the same things."

Then you take action. In the Bible, it says prayer without actions is dead. Our faith without actions is dead. So then you take action. This is called the *principle of reversibility*: if you act as if you already believe that you are meant to be a big success, then you will start to feel and believe it. The action will create the feeling, just as the feeling creates the action.

William James of Harvard, the founder of American psychology, said that if you want to be self-confident, act as if you already are self-confident, and the action will create the emotion. This is the way we start to eliminate those self-limiting beliefs. We first start to challenge them, and then we do the opposite of what a person would do if they had this belief.

What if I had all the self-confidence in the world? What if I was not afraid of anything? If I could knock on any door, talk to anybody, how would I behave? I would get up early in the morning, and I'd go out there and knock on every door and ring every telephone, visit every customer, as if I were in a desperate race to see as many people as possible. And if you do that, surprise, surprise—you develop the same level of confidence as a person who is already extraordinarily successful.

Dan

Excellent. Talk about how our expectations about what we can accomplish play such a big role in what we actually accomplish. I'm thinking of a person who goes into a situation with the expectation that it's going to be very grueling, with long hours, and so forth, as opposed to someone with a more open, positive mind-set.

I know you've talked about studies that have been done on expectations showing that if you hold high expectations, with a very high bar, people will actually go much farther than with a low bar. So talk about how people can set high expectations for an outcome, as they begin an event, to give them a greater chance of success.

Brian

I began teaching this subject thirty-five years ago after thousands of hours of research, and I found that there is a series of mental laws. The first mental law is *the law of cause and effect*. This law says that for every effect in your life, there is a cause or causes. If you can duplicate those causes, you can achieve the effect.

So, again, if you want to double your income, what is it that people who are earning twice as much as you do all day long that's different from what you're doing? If you want to know, go and ask them, "What are you doing differently from me?" Whatever they tell you, do it, and do it over and over again. Do it without question.

I took karate for ten years. I got a black belt in two different fields. In karate, when you start off, you do exactly what you're told to do, and you do it hundreds of times, and then thousands of times. In that first half of every karate class, you go back to basics, and you repeat the basics—punching, kicking, moving sideways, forward, backwards. You do that for the first half of the class. In the second half, you do more advanced things, like free fighting. And you do it all over and over and over again. You do it thousands of times until, when you get into competition, it's absolutely automatic. You don't even have to think to act. But you always follow exactly what you're told at the beginning.

It's the same thing if you want to become an athlete. You do exactly what the coach tells you. If you want to become a musician, you do what the music teachers tell you. If you want to do anything, you do the cause, and the effect will follow. So the effect that you desire is to double your income. What are the causes of earning twice as much? The first rule is that if you do what other successful people do, because of the law of cause and effect, you soon get the same results they do. There's no mystery.

The second principle is *the law of belief.* The law of belief says that whatever you believe with feeling, with conviction, becomes your reality. It's the intensity of your beliefs that creates the reality.

Say you're told that you're going to meet a very successful person. This person has started with nothing. They're worth a hundred million dollars, but they are very humble. They don't dress as if they're wealthy or anything, and they don't like to talk about their background. You're introduced to that person and you believe that this person is rich and smart and talented and everything else. How would you treat that person? Well, you'd be a little bit awestruck, you'd be respectful, you'd listen to whatever they say. They could say, "Yes, it's a warm day today, maybe we're going to have a warm summer." You think, "Oh geez, he's going to get into the commodity market. Maybe he's going to tie up pork bellies or orange juice futures." Whatever this person said, you think there's brilliance to it. You've got to listen to it carefully; take notes. So the law of belief says that whatever you believe with feeling becomes your reality.

The third law is called *the law of expectations*. The law of expectations says that whatever you expect with confidence becomes your own self-fulfilling prophecy, and there are libraries full of examples. In fact there was a complete article on expectations theory in one of the email newsletters yesterday. It says that there are four areas of expectations.

The first area is the expectations of your parents. There are two factors that build happy, healthy, self-confident kids that grow up and become winners and achievers in life. The first factor is a democratic environment: the children's opinions are respected and solicited. They talk together and they listen, and the family does what one or more of the kids want to do.

We used to go out for dinner with our kids when they were

three, four, five, six. We'd say, "Where would you like to go for dinner? It's your turn to choose." They would choose where we would go for dinner. The next time we went out, I'd ask the next child, "Where would you like to go? You're in charge. You're the leader," and they would say, "I want to go here."

They have grown up believing that their opinions are valuable, because everybody in their family, including these two giants, the parents, have listened to them, supported them 100%. By the time my kids were ten or eleven, and were speaking to adults, they expected to be listened to, and they expected to be able to respond and answer. Adults would shake their heads. "I'm speaking to this ten-year-old who has to stand on a chair so they can make eye contact with me as if he or she was an adult."

The second area of expectations is the expectations of your boss. You'll find the bosses with high expectations are the ones that build the most peak performance work environments. The boss expects people to do well, absolutely believes in it.

The third area is the expectations that you have of the people who look up to you. People will always rise. Your children, your spouse, your friends, your employees will always rise to your level of expectations. If you have high, positive expectations for them, they will not disappoint you. They will rise to that.

The fourth area is the expectations you have of yourself. You can never be greater or more successful on the outside than you expect yourself to be on the inside.

I sometimes use this little example. Imagine that there was a computer store and you could go and you could buy an operating program, and you could slide it into your brain, and your brain would operate on that program for the rest of your life. What would be the best program for you to buy? The answer is this: buy the program that says that you are going to be a great success in life. You program that into your brain so that no matter what happens in life, you expect to succeed, you expect to learn, you expect to benefit, you expect to prosper; no matter what happens, you'll just come right back again.

That's why you see that many people will lose their fortunes, millions, even billions of dollars. Two or three years later, they're back, and they're worth millions and billions of dollars. What on earth happened? Their belief was solid, because they knew how to do it. Their expectations were totally 100%, and this mental set was more powerful than all the facts in the world. So your expectations determine your actions. Your expectations determine your attitude. Earl Nightingale said that *attitude* is the most important word in the language.

Your attitude toward other people—is it positive, are you cheerful, are you warm, are you genial, are you friendly, do you have high energy? If you expect to be successful and you expect to be liked, and you expect to learn something from every setback, then your attitude is going to be positive, which everyone will tell you is the foundation principle for success in life.

Finally, your attitude determines your actions. It starts with your *values*, what you believe is important. It then spreads to your *beliefs*, because your values determine your beliefs about reality, which then go out like a target, getting wider. The next circle out is your *expectations*. Your beliefs determine your expectations, your expectations determine your attitude, and your attitude determines your actions, and your actions determine your results.

So it starts with your values. Who are you really inside? What do you believe and care about? That determines your beliefs and everything else.

Dan

Outstanding. Some people feel that beliefs are so deeply ingrained that any kind of conscious programming couldn't overcome them. I know that over the past several years, psychology has moved away from the Freudian concept of repression and the idea that you need years of psychoanalysis to exorcise the demon from within.

As you talked about earlier, Martin Seligman's concept of positive psychology has now been studied and shown to be accurate. It says that one can change one's beliefs by practicing new thoughts and actions. Talk about why one can change one's beliefs, and counteract this Freudian idea that these things lie so deep down that you can't even be aware of them; instead you have to go through the analysis of the subconscious for years and years to get rid of them.

Brian

It's the principle that we talked about earlier. It's called the *act as if principle*. You say, "I want to have purely positive beliefs. I want to have a belief that I am destined to be a great success in life. If that were already true, how would I behave differently?" Act as if you were already the person that you desire to be. The actions will create the feelings, and the feelings will create the actions, and the actions will create the results.

The way we get rid of a self-limiting belief is we replace it with a positive and life-enhancing belief. So I say, "I don't believe in myself," or "I don't have enough confidence," or "I'm not smart enough, or attractive enough." Those are the negative beliefs,

The positive belief is "I have more brainpower than I could ever use in my lifetime. It's just a matter of getting it out. I have the same unlimited ability to succeed that anybody else has. I'm an attractive and a popular person. That's the belief that I choose to have." Then act as if you already had that belief. It wears down the old belief. Eventually the old belief is sent down to the basement, put in a box, and packed away, and the new belief comes to dominate your life.

Dan

Is it accurate to say that we can reprogram our beliefs almost like a computer? As a human beings, in many ways we are much more complex than a computer is. But there are people out there who claim, "I can teach you how to reprogram your beliefs in hours, or minutes." It's the idea that, if you can do it in days or years, you can do it in minutes or hours. It's a quick-fix approach to reprogramming beliefs. Where do you come down on this idea of reprogramming?

Brian

If it takes you a lifetime to develop a self-limiting belief, it's very doubtful that you will switch it in a matter of minutes or hours. Let's imagine that you consider yourself to be a loser or a poor player in a sport and you win first place. That's not going to automatically cause yourself to see yourself as a first-place winner for the rest of your life. You're going to backslide because of the comfort zone. You'll slip back into the old way of thinking. So when you do have a success, the key is to replay it in your mind.

You see, before every event of importance, every person creates a visual picture of how they're going to perform. Sometimes it's clear, sometimes it's fuzzy, but it's always a visual picture. The person you see is the person you'll be.

So you can take a previous success experience, an experience that was connected with an emotion of pride or joy or excitement or happiness: you won a prize, you got an award, someone had a surprise party for you. You did something that was really good, and you still remember. You still beam about how successful it was. You can then take a picture of an upcoming event and simultaneously remember that happy event. What happens is the two are connected in your subconscious mind, so you feel happy, confident, successful about the upcoming event. Then you just walk in.

Athletes do this all the time. Before they go on stage, actors, singers, performers create a visual picture of themselves performing at their best. We call this *conditioning*. There's a form of athletic conditioning that's used by all the top athletes in the world. Sitting quietly in a chair, or lying in bed, they visualize themselves performing their sport perfectly.

Figure skaters use this technique. They'll put on the music that they're going to skate by. They will let the music play, and they'll skate through their entire routine in their mind. They do this over and over before they go to sleep and get up in the morning. Then, when they go out, they skate absolutely beautifully, because the wonderful thing is, in your mind, you never fall. Your picture is of perfect skating. There are all kinds of stories about people who have never performed a sport before, but they're taught to visualize how to perform it and they did a great job.

One of the greatest, most profound discoveries in all of human history, which Earl Nightingale called "the strangest secret," is that *you become what you think about most of the time.* Just as we say you become what you eat (and everybody agrees with that), so you become what you think about. If you think about yourself in positive, uplifting, genial, humorous terms, that becomes your reality.

Dan

How, then, do positive and helpful belief systems help to turn on a person's action mechanisms? How are beliefs so intricately connected to action, to actually making changes in someone's life?

Brian

If you believe that you're going to be successful, you're very eager to get out there and do it. If you doubt that you're going to be successful, you will procrastinate. Let's talk about salespeople. Salespeople usually have terrible call reluctance, what we call *fear of rejection.* The reason is they believe if they call someone, they're going to be rejected. The person is going to say, "No, I'm not interested" and slam down the phone. So they think about that. They play the picture of the last really rude person who tore a strip off them when they called. As they approach the telephone, they start to think about that rude person, and they start to imagine there's another rude person on the end and they're just about to be dumped on again when they call.

Over time they become more and more fearful of calling, until finally they can't call at all. Most people drop out of sales, not because of lack of success, but because they cannot take the rejection. Part of the rejection, maybe all of it, comes because they expect to be rejected, just like the story I told you about the gentlemen selling cellular telephones in a mall.

He didn't realize it, but after he'd been rejected ten or twenty or fifty times, he expected the next person to reject him as well. But when he changed his thinking—that no, this next person is going to buy from me, because this is a good deal, and they need it, and it will really help them—it transformed his behavior. It wasn't the product, it wasn't the customer, it wasn't the market. It was he himself, who had this tremendous doubt that came from the earlier rejection.

So, it's the same thing as always with us. Do you know that song, "It's Me, O Lord, Standing in the Need of Prayer"? It's we who have to build those positive beliefs, and the way you build it is by doing it.

If you want to climb a mountain, and you want to say, "I climb mountains," climb one. And for the rest of your life, you can say, "I climbed that mountain. Yes, I climb high mountains." It's really hard to climb a high mountain, but afterwards you can say, "I do it." For the rest of your life, you absolutely believe with 100% confidence that you can do it.

That's the key. You act your way into believing. You do the things that you would do if you already had the positive belief, and then it becomes automatic.

Martin Seligman and others are building what they call the *positive psychology field*. Thirty-five years ago they called this *cognitive psychology*. This is another way of saying that you become what you think about most of the time, and there's only one thing in the world that you can control and that's your thinking. So if you think about what you want, and you think about yourself as your very best person and you think about success and achievement and positive results, that's how you will behave. That's how you'll perform.

Remember that wonderful quote from Napoleon Hill, author of *Think and Grow Rich*: "Whatever the mind of man can conceive, and believe, it can achieve." That one quote has transformed the lives of millions of people. Realize it. If I believe it strongly enough and then I back it up with hard, hard work, it becomes my reality. It becomes the truth for me, and once it is, it wipes away and replaces all negative beliefs from the past.

Dan

Excellent. Let's focus on one specific issue and see how you would guide a person to address it in terms of changing their belief. I'll focus on public speaking, since you're a professional public speaker.

Studies show that most people fear public speaking more than death itself. Suppose there is a person who says, "Brian, as part of my job, I have been promoted and I need to do more public speaking, but I am petrified. I am a terrible public speaker. But if I am going to succeed, I need to develop a new belief about myself as being a competent and effective public speaker." What should this person do to become an effective public speaker in a reasonable amount of time?

Brian

Everybody already *is* an effective public speaker. When you sit down with your friends at work, or you go out for lunch, or you have a date, or you have a family get-together, you speak fluently, confidently, competently, clearly. People respond to you in a positive way. People laugh, joke, give you feedback.

So one thing I teach in my speaking academy is to speak to others as though you would speak to a family member across the family dinner table or breakfast table. Imagine you've seen a good movie and you've sat down with a friend. You say, "Have you seen this movie?" "No." "Let me tell you about this movie. It is really, really good. It starts off like this and you really don't know what's going to happen, and this happens. I saw it last night. It was just phenomenal."

Public speech has an opening, a development, a close, and a resolution. When you stand up to speak in front of other people, you take that same thought: that you're just speaking to family members across the dinner table, and you're sharing with them some thoughts, ideas, experiences that you really enjoyed and that they might enjoy as well. That's why they say never speak on a subject that you don't believe in and care about, because it's how you come across emotionally that's going to connect with your audience.

Then plan and prepare. Have a good opening, develop your talk with three key points, and then always have a close. Wrap it up by saying, "The most important thing I learned from this experience was this, and if I have learned it, you can learn it too. Good luck." Something like that.

There's always an opening, a middle, and a close, and all the books and articles ever written on public speaking will say the same things. Elbert Hubbard was one of the greatest authors in American history. He lived in Rochester, New York and he wrote books, sometimes series of books. I have one of his twenty-two volume series, where he took great orators, great singers, great explorers, adventurers, musicians, writers, poets, novelists, military leaders, twenty-two books full, jammed full of detailed stories of the top people throughout history in these areas. And then he turned to writing again. He wrote so much, and so prolifically, that he had to buy a printing press to publish and print all of his books. They're all best sellers. Even today, they're considered heirlooms, antiques. And they're so profound, with so much information.

People would come to him and say, "Mr. Hubbard, I want to be a great writer. I want to be a writer like you. What's the key?" He would say, "The only way to learn to write is to write and write and write." So when I teach my students in speaking, I say the only way to learn to speak is to speak and speak and speak. As you start off, they say it'll take 300 free talks before you are ever able to give your first paid talk.

Some people, like Zig Ziglar, said they made 3000 free talks—mostly sales training for people within his company—before he was ever invited to speak for money. So the only way to learn to speak is to speak and speak. Every time you do it, your fears become fewer and fewer and your confidence grows and grows. Soon you reach the point where you are very confident in speaking. People applaud you. They look up to you, and they shake your hand afterwards and say what a great message that was. And all of your fears disappear.

Your belief now is that you are a qualified and confident speaker. If you've given it enough time to plan and prepare, you can do a great job, and everybody will be happy.

Dan

So, Brian, is there one key thought that you'd like to leave people with about the power of beliefs?

Brian

Everyone turns out to have one big negative belief that holds them back more than anything else. I told you about my thousands of hours of research into negative emotions. What we find is that everyone has one big negative emotion, negative belief, negative idea, based on a previous experience or something that happened to them, something they did or didn't do, something that someone said. Usually it's unclear, which is why in psychiatry, it takes between six months and six years, meeting with a patient once a week for fifty minutes, to help them get it out, to finally identify what's holding them back. What's the lump, what's the block within the psyche that's holding you back? Sometimes it takes a long time for a person to reach the point of clarity and courage where they can tell the psychologist, "This is my problem. This is what happened to me. This is how I reacted." You've seen all this in the movies.

But each person can become their own psychologist. Ninety-nine percent of people do not need professional help. What they need is the ability to think through and say, "What is the one big negative idea or experience that's affecting my beliefs?" Sometimes you can talk it out with your spouse or a good friend, or with a coach or a minister or someone else. But until you can identify that one thing, that one negative belief or experience that's holding you back, you're locked in place. As soon as you can, you are liberated. Suddenly you're free, and it's gone forever.

FOUR

The Problem with Goals:
How to Turn Goal Setting
into Goal Achievement

Dan

Brian, you've become world renowned for teaching people, not only how to set goals and how to set the proper goals, but also how to turn them into achievements. Before we get to what I call the problem with goals, why don't you begin by discussing why goals are essential to being a motivated and successful person throughout your life?

Brian

Imagine that you start off in life, as young people do, with a lot of confusion and uncertainty. Who am I? What do I do? Where do I go? The great questions: what do I do with my life? What do I really want to do with my life?

Most people have no idea when they're young. I equate it to setting off across a strange country with no road map and no road signs. How long would it take you to get anywhere if you don't have a clear destination and you have no road map and no road signs?

Imagine you were driving in a foreign city, like London, or Amsterdam, or Paris, and there were no signs anywhere. You could just drive around. That's what 80% of the population do: they just drive around and end up back at home every night.

Eventually they come to the conclusion that there's really nothing they can do. They've developed one of the most terrible of all human maladies. It's called *learned helplessness.* Learned helplessness is a major reason why people don't succeed, they feel helpless, they feel there's nothing they can do. It's because they have not succeeded greatly in the past. They just assume that, as Shakespeare said, "Past is prologue." What has happened in the past is what's going to happen in the future, so they lose their enthusiasm for goals.

I'll often ask my audiences, "How many people here have goals?" Every hand goes up. I say, "Well, that's pretty surprising, because according to the studies, only 3% of people have goals. Everybody here has their hand up. So what are your goals?"

I'll ask them. "Well, I want to be happy," and somebody says, "I want to be rich," and someone says, "I want to find the right person," "I want to travel," "I want to learn new skills," "I want to make a lot of money," and so on.

I realized many years ago that people don't have goals, they have wishes. The definition of a wish is a goal with no energy behind it. I say it's like a bullet with no powder in the cartridge.

People go through life shooting blanks, they shoot and it goes click, click, because there's no energy behind it. That's why I began studying goal setting when I was twenty-five. We know that in life, each person has turning points; I hope that this book will be a turning point for some of our readers.

You're going through life, and you come to a point where something happens, and you go in a different direction. You may walk into a party and meet another person that you've never seen before. You fall in love, get married, you're together for the rest of your lives. You may move to a different city or a different country, and you have a life together. If you hadn't gone to that party (and you were thinking of maybe not going), you wouldn't have met the person; your life would have been different.

It's a great entertainment, by the way, to help people to go back and find their turning points. One of the great turning points for me was when I discovered goals. Then I realized that people who think that they have goals really only have wishes, and as a result they never set goals.

Three percent of the population have clear goals. But if you think you have a goal, then you have no need to set any goals. "Oh, I've got goals, I know what I want to do." Then there are even people out there who say you don't need goals. All you need to do is listen to your heart, follow your instincts, do whatever you feel like doing, and let it all hang out, and everything else will come to you.

I strongly disagree. These people are either failures themselves, or they've already achieved success by setting and working on their goals aggressively for twenty-five years. I know both sides; I know both types of people. I know very wealthy people who, at the beginning of their careers, worked like dogs, worked on goals, got up early and stayed late. They have struggled, and strived, and sweated seven days a week, and finally they break through. Then they say, "Oh, this is cute. You don't really need to have goals. All you need to do is have happy thoughts and think happy things, and sit at home, and money will come to your mailbox," like in *The Secret*.

Goals give you a track to run on, goals give you a sense of direction, goals give you a feeling of clarity. Goals enable you to concentrate your energies and to focus on a single thing. Goals enable you to accomplish vastly more in a year or two than many people accomplish in five or ten years.

Dan

There are people who have gone to seminars, and over the years they've written down lists of goals they're going to achieve. The problem is that there's a big difference between this idea of "I'm going to set these goals" and what it takes to actually turn it into goal achievement. At the beginning of the year, we know that health clubs become rich on people who have all these resolutions for their health that they don't follow through on.

Talk about that difference, because goal achievement is much more of a long-term process. What is your program for longer-term goal achievement once someone has written out what they really want in life? What steps do people need to take in going from where they are to realization?

Brian

Very few people go to seminars and set goals and then nothing happens. In almost every case, if you go to a seminar or workshop and are basically forced, because everybody's doing it, to write down your goals and make plans for their accomplishment, you're astonished at how much more you accomplish and how fast.

I have a little goal-setting process, which I teach to my audiences. It's life transforming. I developed this system based on years of work. I'm the best-selling author in the world on goals in twenty-five languages, according to my publisher. I sell books in every major language in virtually every major country in the world and in many minor countries, so I know a lot about the subject.

Here are the seven key steps. Step number one is for you to sit down with a piece of paper and decide exactly what you want. Decide exactly what you want to have in life without limitations. Imagine that whatever you write down as a goal, you can have. The only limit on what you can accomplish is what you write down, clearly, on paper.

That's number one: *be specific.* The rule is that your goal should be so clear and specific that a six-year-old child could understand your goal and then could tell you how close you are to it. This is why "I want to be happy," "I want to be rich," "I want to travel" fail the goal test. Nobody could ever figure out what those mean. Are you there, or how far away are you?

Step number two is to *write it down.* A goal that is not in writing is only a fantasy. As I said before, it's a wish, it's an illusion, because there's something about writing down a goal that triggers what psychologists call a psycho-neuro-motor activity. *Psycho-* is your mind; you think about the goal when you're writing it; *neuro-* means you are evaluating it in your mind; and *motor* means that you're actually using your hand and your body to write it down.

When you write down a goal, you trigger your visual learning modality, because you see it. You trigger your audio modality because you say it sub-vocally to yourself as you write it down, and you trigger your kinesthetic ability because it takes the movement of your physical body to write it. There have been a whole series of studies on why students who take notes during class are vastly more successful in their grades than students who take no notes or who type their notes. When you're writing things down, you're actually transferring the written goal to your subconscious mind. Your subconscious mind is now going to work before you even get up. It works twenty-four hours a day to bring that goal into your life. Writing down your goals is one of the most extraordinary things I ever learned in my life, a major turning point.

Step number three is to *set a deadline*. Set a specific date and tell your subconscious mind that you want the goal by this time. If it's a long-term goal, then break it down. If it's a five-year goal, break it down into five one-year goals. Then, from a one-year goal, break it down to three-month goals, and then one-month goals, and then one-week goals.

Many people, especially in sales and marketing, will break it down into one-day goals. Sometimes they'll break it down into one-hour goals. If I want to achieve this goal, which is financial independence five years from now, this is what I'm going to have to do every hour of every day. They're very clear, and they discipline themselves just to do what lies clearly at hand.

I love that quote from Thomas Carlyle: "Our great job in life is not to see what lies dimly at a distance, but to do what lies clearly at hand." Successful people do what lies clearly at hand. They do the most important thing now, and they get it done, they get on with it. Unsuccessful people always have an excuse to procrastinate, to put it off to later. They check their email, or they send a text, or they go and talk to someone and have a cup of coffee. In the back of their minds they really mean well; they have good intentions. What is the road to hell paved with? It's good intentions.

As the great economist Ludwig von Mises said, "Only action is action. Not talk, not wish, not hope, not intention, only action is action." That's number three, decide what you want, write it down, set a deadline.

Step number four is to *make a list* of everything that you could possibly do to achieve the goal. Keep adding to the list until the list is complete.

There's something about writing down every step that transforms your thinking about the goal. Let's say your goal is to double your income. Holy smokes, I'm going to double my income in twelve months?

It's so enormous, but then you say, "What would be all the things that I would need to do to double my income?" You begin to write them down. I need to upgrade my skills in this area, or I need to read this book, or go to this course, or listen to this CD, watch this program, go onto YouTube and see if I can't find some of the top sales people giving their ideas (which people do). These are the things I'd have to do every day if I wanted to upgrade my knowledge and skills and achieve my goal. Just keep writing them down. You'll be astonished.

Step number five is *you take your list and you organize the list into a plan*. The way you organize your list into a plan is you create a checklist. A checklist is one the great miracles of modern success. People who use checklists accomplish five or ten times as much as people without checklists.

This is a list of every single step in order. What is step number one to achieve my goal? What is step number two; what is step number three? I was giving a seminar in Sydney, Australia, and this young entrepreneur, who was about twenty-six years old, came up to me and said, "I don't know how to achieve my goal." I said, "What is your goal?"

He said, "I want to sell my business. I started this business when I was nineteen. I've been working at it now for seven years. It's successful, it makes good money, but I've always wanted to travel and see the world. I want to go out and do something. I'm twenty-six, and I don't want to find myself working for the rest of my life. I'm still single. I just want to sell my business and travel."

I said, "What have you done?" He said, "I talk to people, I ask people, I just don't know." I said, "Why don't you go to the bookstore and get a book entitled *How to Sell Your Business*? An enormous number of entrepreneurs have written books on that title or something like it. *How to Sell a Business in Ninety Days, Keys to Selling Your Business.*"

He said, "Are there books on this subject?" I said, "Absolutely, tens of thousands of businesses are sold every year by successful entrepreneurs to others who want to pick up and carry on." At the lunch break he went across the street to the bookstore, and bought two books on how to sell your business.

He said, "I've never seen this stuff. How you put together financial statements, how you advertise, how you position, how you find interest groups and different industries." Two months later, he wrote me a letter. He said, "I sold my business. I got a great price. I have all the money I need. My ticket is paid for. I'm leaving for Europe, I'm going to see the world. It was amazing."

My point was that if you want to sell your business, the first thing you do is get a book on how to sell a business. If you want to double your sales, then get a book on how to increase your sales. If you want to manage your time better, then get a book on that subject.

The first thing you do—it's like starting an engine—vroom, vroom. You start the engine. Taking the first step is almost like pushing off when you're skiing. Suddenly you're in motion, and suddenly you're moving forward, and now you're gaining speed and you go faster. The momentum principle kicks in, and you start to get this feeling of progress. You become exhilarated by taking the first step.

Make a list of all the things that you have to do and put them in sequence. Step number six is *take the first step.* I believe that in life, all success comes from taking the first step. This is why Confucius, the wisest philosopher in Chinese history, said, "A journey of a thousand leagues begins with a single step." Taking the first step is the hardest thing of all.

Sometimes I say, "How many people in this audience have books at home that they bought and they intend to read someday?" Everybody. "Well, here's what you do. You go back and you pick up the book and you read the first chapter. You buy a book, just read the first chapter. If that doesn't get you going into the book, it's fine, you've given it your best shot."

Ninety percent of business books are not read beyond the first chapter. Why is that? Because after reading the first chapter, people come to the conclusion that this is not that helpful, it's not that good, it's not that well-written. Read the first chapter. It transforms your life to get an idea and take the first step.

All success comes from taking the first step in any area. Step number seven in goal setting, which is going to make you rich, happy, popular, and thin, is *do something every day on your major goal.* Do something every day, whether it's something small or something large. Read something, learn something, do something, but every day keep the plate spinning, keep the momentum going, keep moving.

The momentum principle of success also says that if you stop moving towards your goal, it's very hard to start moving again. It's very hard to get up the energy and the gumption and the time and everything else. But if you keep moving towards your goal, it's much easier to keep moving. It's one of the greatest of all principles of success: continuous motion.

Here's the exercise. Take a clean sheet of paper and write down ten goals that you would like to accomplish in the next twelve months. Twelve-month goals are more powerful than two-, or five-, or ten-year goals. You can write on another sheet of paper that you want to make a million dollars in ten years; that's fine. But keep the focus on twelve months: twelve months you can see, twelve months you can work on, twelve months you can focus on.

Write down ten goals, but write them in using the three P's. Your subconscious mind is really very much like a child, it's simple and it's innocent, and it can only accept commands that are very simple, like giving them to a child. The commands are very simple, the first P is *personal*, so you always begin a goal with the word *I. I earn, I achieve, I sell, I drive, I live in.* Whatever the goal is, it's *I* plus an action verb. That's what activates your subconscious mind and starts it to work like a motorcycle engine.

Step number two is make it *positive*. Never say *I stop smoking, I quit smoking, I stop doing this, I lose this number of pounds.* Always say *I weigh this number of pounds* and so on.

Step number three is make it *present tense*, because your subconscious mind cannot process a command unless it's in the present tense. So you say *I earn this amount of money* and then write *by this date.* Give it a use-by date, as we say. *I earn this amount of money by December 31,* and whatever year it is. I weigh this number of pounds by this date, at the end of a particular month. Your subconscious mind loves time pressure.

Your subconscious mind then goes to work twenty-four hours a day to move you toward the goal and to attract the goal toward you. Everybody's used this. I've taught this to more than a million people in seventy-five countries. They come back to me over and over again, a year later, two, three years later, and they say, "You changed my life. You made me rich. I was struggling, I was going nowhere, I was in debt, I was broke, I lost my job, and then you changed my life, you made me rich." I said, "What is it in my materials that achieved this goal?" They said, "It was the goals, it was always the goals, that exercise."

I gave this exercise to a very wealthy man recently. After I left, he wrote down ten goals. He said, "The goals started to materialize almost as I was writing. The phone rang, people came in. It was miraculous." He could not believe how fast the goals were achieved. They were one-year goals, but they started to be reached almost immediately.

Sometimes people say, "What if it doesn't work?" I say, "No, that's the wrong question. The right question is what if it *does* work? It just cost you a piece of paper, and a pen, and five minutes of your time. Is that so much?"

In my seminars, I'll say, "Now imagine that we have a magic wand and that you can achieve all the goals you wrote down sooner or later if you still want them badly enough. But with this magic wand, you have a special wish. You can achieve any one goal on that list within twenty-four hours. The question is, what one goal, if you achieved it, would have the greatest positive impact on your life? What one goal, if you achieved it within twenty-four hours, would change your life more than anything else?"

In goals, you find there are inputs and outputs. A person wants to have a big house, but what would enable them to have a big house would be a certain level of income. You say, "I earn this amount of money so I can have this house, and this car, and take this trip," and so on.

Start off with the one goal that would have the biggest positive impact on all your other goals. Put a circle around that, then take a clean sheet of paper and write it down. Positive, present tense, personal: *I achieve this goal by this date.* Then make a list of everything that you can do to achieve that one goal. Then organize this list by sequence. What do you do first? What do you second? and so on. Then take action on your list and do something every day.

If you'll do that, you'll transform your life almost like a miracle. I've given this exercise to a million or two million people. Not one person has ever said to me it doesn't work. They only come back with stories, extraordinary stories after years of struggle: suddenly they're wealthy. Suddenly they have big beautiful homes and their businesses are growing, and they've met different people; they've traveled and they're learning new languages.

They come back and they're just, as young people say, "smh"— shaking my head. They just could not believe how powerful it was. It's almost as if they were struck by some kind of positive lightning.

If I could only give people one piece of advice, it would be this: to write down your goals in this method. We talked earlier about personal responsibility. Accepting personal responsibility is the starting point of becoming an adult. A good friend of mine says that until you accept responsibility, you're still a child. You're still blaming all your problems on someone else. When you cross the line and accept responsibility, you become an adult for the first time.

Then the next question is, responsibility for what? The answer is, responsibility for your goals. Now you say, "All right, I'm responsible. What am I going to do with all this responsibility? I'm going to achieve these goals."

Dan

That's great. Let's say you are somebody who has achieved something significant. I'm thinking here of people who are very successful and goal oriented at a young age. Then they lose their motivation to succeed at an older age.

I'm thinking of the celebrity who gains great fame as an actor in his or her teens. Commonly they hit their twenties and thirties, and by forty they're broke and addicted to drugs or something like that. Then there's the athlete who's dominant up until their thirties, and after retiring, after the age of fifty, they've committed suicide or they're broke. There are very few people like the Roger Staubachs, who go off to have successful business careers.

What's going on here? Discuss how this reflects the fact that the goal achievement process must continue throughout our lives. It can help us reinvent our lives when we need to at different points.

Brian

To start with the subject of reinvention, I'm probably the only author in the world who's written a book on that. Published by American Management Association of New York, it's called *Reinvention,* and it talks about what do you do when your life changes, when there's turmoil, when your career ends, or your industry ends. How do you reinvent yourself? You go back to writing down your goals. What would I do if my life were perfect? What would I do differently from today? Where do I want to be in five or ten years?

For those people who come apart after early success, there are different reasons and different categories. With actors and actresses, 95% of them are unemployed at any given time. To get a job as an actor or an actress is a tremendous break. You must know the right people, you must be in the right time at the right place, you must take hundreds of bit parts and be discovered to get a non-bit part. You must do that part so well that you're given a supporting role. You must do everything really well, and then it's very possible that you won't work for another five years.

You could think of all kinds of actors who haven't had a job for five years, and all their expenses keep going. I remember James Caan, who got an Academy Award for *The Godfather.* He became very selective. His agent blew smoke in his ear that he was so good, he was so popular, he didn't have to take anything but the very best roles, so he turned down some of the very best roles in Hollywood. He turned down *Tootsie.* He was the first choice for *Tootsie,* which won two Academy Awards. He turned down a couple of these roles, and he ended up living in a one-bedroom apartment with two dogs in Hollywood, because he ran out of money.

Of course, if you don't have any money, they don't invite you to parties. If you're not in roles, they don't invite you. You can't take any trips, and you just keep going out day after day, week after week, auditioning for a part, any part, because it's the only way you have to make money. What happens with show business people when their career fades?

Sometimes they can irritate somebody, and that person will just put a black mark on them, and nobody will hire them. They said something, they did something, it happens all the time. Now the only skill you have that got you out of the ditch in the first place is your ability to act, and there's no work.

That's what causes people to go downhill. Of course in Hollywood, in the entertainment industry, you're surrounded with drugs. You get drugs as easily as you can get chewing gum. Then people learn that this guy's on drugs, taking cocaine and other things. Don't touch him with a ten-foot pole. If you're going to invest millions of dollars in a movie, you can't risk having one of the actors not show up with the crew there and everything else. It costs a fortune. So their career just goes into the ditch.

Most actors and actresses are fighting with self-esteem issues. They're compensating for what happened to them as children. They're trying to escape that by earning the adulation of strangers, people who have never seen them before and will never see them again. These people will crawl over broken glass to please these people; then they become arrogant, they become condescending, they become ridiculous.

Sports—mostly poor people get into sports. Even if they're successful, their bodies only last for a certain period of time. They've never developed any other skills, so there's nothing they can do. There are some people like Roger Staubach: while they're playing, they're learning, they're taking extra courses during the off season. They're planning for their careers when they finish football, they're putting money aside, and they're investing carefully. When their career comes to an end, which it does, they're ready, they're set. They've got new opportunities, they have job offers, they've already begun making their transition plans.

With regard to entrepreneurs, here's an interesting point. You never hear of this drug addiction, alcoholism, declining into apathy, and so on in Silicon Valley.

Why is that? It's because they're so busy all the time. They're active, they have goals. They're making steps forward, they're accomplishing things, they're changing from product to product and company to company, starting new stuff and closing down old stuff. I'm sure there are lots of drugs out there, just like alcohol, but you don't hear about people who make a lot of money in high-tech who suddenly fall apart and become hopeless drug addicts. No, they're doing new stuff. They've got this: *I succeeded, and I succeeded based on my own hard efforts. I succeeded in competition with thousands of other people, and I want to compete.* They're surrounded by people who are positive and upbeat and motivated, who've got goals and energy and everything else.

It's the same thing with entrepreneurs. You very seldom see a successful entrepreneur who makes his money and becomes successful and then falls apart. They're in the groove. They are working, they are rolling and strolling, they are doing new stuff. I've met entrepreneurs who are billionaires and multibillionaires. All they think about is the next business, the next opportunity, the next product, the next service. They don't fall apart and drink.

Look at a certain presidential candidate, whose name will not be mentioned. He doesn't smoke, doesn't drink—no one in his family smokes or drinks—he exercises, lives a clean life and so on. They've been wealthy for decades now—no trace of falling apart.

The thing that keeps you going is that you always have something to look forward to. The most important thing in life is always to have something to look forward to. When people don't have anything to look forward to, they lose hope. Hope is really the great motivator of the human being. Hope for a better future through your own efforts.

Dan

Outstanding, and that brings back the brilliance of that comment from Earl Nightingale: that success is the progressive realization of a worthy goal. It changes your paradigm, because when people think, "Once I get that one goal, then I'm a success." If you just fixate on that, you're no longer a success, because you're sitting on past achievements, you have nothing that you're working toward. This is a great reminder for all of us that even when we are successful and the broader world acknowledges that we're successful, we have to continually reinvent ourselves. We have to continue this process throughout our lives.

I'm wondering if you could discuss a story or two of well-known individuals you've known. We don't have to name names. People who just really lacked motivation or focus in their early lives, and then used your goal achievement system to achieve a level of success beyond their wildest dreams. This is just to give readers additional hope that this system doesn't discriminate. Anybody who puts it to work, regardless of background, regardless of what advantages they're starting off with in life—if they follow this diligently, they, too, can be successful.

Brian

It's a great question, because I have people come up to me like a river in every seminar who have been to my previous seminars. They tell wonderful success stories. Almost invariably, as with the example I gave you of the young guy who made the videotape, is they learned the importance of self-esteem. They learned that they could control their own self-esteem. They could regulate it, and they could turn it up by simply repeating *I like myself* enthusiastically and with conviction.

I teach my audiences when you get up in the morning, say, "I like myself and I love my work. I like myself, I love my work." Like a train getting going: "I like myself, I love my work." You can't say this for more than a few seconds without starting to smile and having blood pour into your brain, releasing endorphins. You just feel happy.

We'll talk about this later, but self-talk, or affirmations, is extraordinarily powerful. It's part of positive psychology, it's been around for centuries. They're just repackaging it now and calling it something different.

The average person speaks to themselves in what is called the *inner dialogue*, at a rate of about 1500 words a minute. It just flows like a fast moving river. If you are not careful, that inner dialogue will be negative. You'll talk about things that you're mad at, things that you're worried about, people that you're irritated with, and so on.

You have to step into the dialogue, deliberately stop it, and speak positively to yourself. The default setting on every human brain is to think about their worries and their pains. You have to click the default setting off by talking to yourself about who you want to be and what you want to accomplish.

I have many examples, and I don't have any negative examples. People who are starting a business, people who have been struggling for a long time, will come up to me and say, "I doubled my income," "I tripled my income." I used to teach a seven-step process for increasing your income ten times in ten years. I have people all over the world who learned that process. They say that it didn't take ten years; it took five, or six. Ten was far too conservative.

I said, "I know, you do it much faster than ten years, but ten years is easier to believe." They said they just practiced it every day. The formula, by the way, is very simple: get up every morning an hour early and read to upgrade your skills. Wealthy people read an hour or two every day. Poor people don't read at all, unless they read the newspapers.

Number two is write down your goals, again, every single day, in a spiral notebook. Every day, without looking at the previous page, rewrite your major goals, just reprogram them into your mind.

Step number three is plan every day in advance. You'll increase you productivity 25% by simply making a list of everything you do before you start.

Number four, focus and concentrate on your most important task. You'll increase your productivity by 50–100% just by starting and completing your most important task first thing every day. It's one of the greatest success principles in history.

Step number five is ask two questions after every single call: *What did I do right? What would I do differently?* After every single event of importance, you do an after-action report: *What did I do right? What would I do differently?* If you do that, if you capture your experience on paper, you'll increase your learning speed by about five or ten times.

Instead of taking years to bring yourself to the point where you're extremely successful, you can do it in a year, just by doing a brief recap of your previous event, whether it was a presentation, a sales call, a negotiation, or a meeting with your banker. What did I do right—because there is always something—and what would I do differently if I were going to do that next time?

These I call the magic questions, because the answers are both positive. When you write down your answers, you program those answers into your subconscious mind, and they become part of your permanent operating system.

Step number six is to listen to audio programs all the time you can, all the time you're moving around. Turn off the radio. We used to say, listen to audiocassettes, and then listen to CDs, but today listen on your iPhone. You can now have hundreds of hours of the best audio learning in the world. Instead of listening to music, turn driving time into learning time. Turn your car into a university on wheels. Never stop taking in new information.

I'm amazed every day, including yesterday. I'm driving along listening to an interview with a successful person, and there's a couple of gems. Then I listened to another interview and said, "Well, here's an idea, another gem." This stuff is valuable. I'll promise you it's going to be worked into my next seminar on Saturday in Budapest. These ideas are great, and one idea can change your whole life.

The last, number seven, is to treat everyone you meet like a million-dollar customer. Treat everyone you meet as though they're the most important person in the world. Treat them with grace, treat them with respect, treat them with pleasantness, cordiality, geniality, courtesy. Be really nice to people.

The most successful people in the world are described by others as nice people. In any language, in any culture, in any nationality, the most successful people are described as nice. Just be nice to people, and every door of opportunity will open up to you.

Dan

Brian, that was a great summary, but if there's one thought that's most essential in this chapter on goals and goal achievement, what would that be?

Brian

It's one of the great success principles. I read an 800-page book by a man named Orison Swett Marden, who was a businessman in the 1890s. He decided to sit down and write a book on success because so many people were succeeding; America was booming. He sat down and wrote a book called *Pushing to the Front.*

He had lost his business and his money, and he was living in a room over a stable, with horses and buggies. He was so happy that he finished this book, piles and piles of handwritten manuscript. He went down the street to treat himself to a steak dinner. He walked down, and he got himself a beer and had a steak dinner, and sat there. While he was sitting there, he heard shouting in the street and a fire alarm. The stable burned to the ground, and his entire manuscript was gone.

His whole book was about people who started with nothing, and through great perseverance and hard work had become really successful. He was sitting there and he said, "The heck with this." Then he said, "Wait a minute; what did I write in my book?"

The two keys to success, he said, are *get-tuitiveness*, and *stick-tuitiveness*. I've just finished a book called *Get Going and Keep Going.* Everything else in between is the process. The key to success is to set a goal and then to get going and keep going, and don't stop until you achieve it.

He went back, and everything was gone. He was completely destitute, and he had a few clothes. He took the clothes and he moved to another city and got another job. He sat down and began rewriting the book from scratch, from memory. He rewrote the whole book. In the meantime, it was the early 1890s, and the country had gone into a depression. Nobody was interested now.

He was at a meeting somewhere, and someone said, "Somebody should write about these success principles so we can get this country going again." He said, "I've written a book like that, but I haven't been able to find a publisher." The other man said, "I've got a couple of publisher friends. Let's take a look at the manuscript."

So they did, and they said, "This is great stuff." It is one of the greatest success books ever written—so inspiring. They published it under the title *Pushing to the Front.*

It became the best-selling book in America. They say this was the book that single-handedly brought America into the twentieth century. His last recommendation was "get going, keep going." That's it.

In the 1890s, Marden founded *Success* magazine, and he wrote a series of books on success. If you can find those books today, they're mind-blowing. They're some of the best books on personal and business success ever written.

FIVE

The Power of Right Action and Flexibility: Why "Just Do It" Is Not Enough Today

Dan

Now we're going to introduce people to a quality that has always been important to success, but probably never more so than in the world we live today, and that's flexibility.

To set the stage, I want to discuss how our globally interconnected, quickly changing world has made Nike's maxim of "Just do it," which they started in the '80s with Michael Jordan, insufficient for remaining motivated and effective today. I'm referring to the fact that actions we take toward our goals today may become ineffective or irrelevant next year if we don't stay on top of the trends. I'm also thinking of people in business who set a goal and go out to achieve it, but they don't adjust for changing trends in the culture, in the marketplace, and so forth.

Can you talk about this idea of right action and flexibility— the idea that we need to adjust along the way and stay attuned to what effect our actions are having in light of the changes going on around us?

Brian

To begin with, the willingness and ability to take action towards your goals is the single most important quality of all. The world is full of talented people with fantasies and dreams, but they don't take action. They always have an excuse not to do it yet. Taking action is very important.

Just as an aside, as I said in my goal setting system *Take Action and Then Do Something Every Day*, when you take action, three things happen. First of all, you get immediate feedback from your actions, which enable you to change course and direction. Number two is you get more ideas, and the ideas are always for more actions that you can take to move ahead faster. And number three, your self-confidence goes up and your self-esteem goes up. You get all three of those benefits from taking action, and you get nothing from sitting there on the couch. So taking action is important.

What we have found in psychology is that once you have decided to achieve a goal, the first action will actually appear, almost like a light on the floor in a nightclub. The first action will always be clear. You can always see the first step. If you take the first step, the second step will appear. And if you take the second step, the third step will appear.

Here's an interesting discovery, as my friend Charlie Jones used to say: nothing works; at least it doesn't work the first time. So when you take action toward a particular goal, be assured that it's not going to work. Peter Drucker says that you need at least four iterations in your direction toward a new goal before you actually hit the right one.

I just read a study in *Harvard Business Review*. One company tried fifteen different methods, fifteen different business models on a new business and a new product, before they found the one that worked. The only thing that matters in life is, does it work, is it getting you the results that you expected? People can fall in love with a course of action even before it's ever worked. Peter Drucker said, "If the American public knew how many mistakes were made in the management suite because of managerial ego, there would be riots in the streets."

In Silicon Valley they have pre-revenue companies, which are companies that have never sold anything. These people are out trying either to sell stock or to raise money. Sometimes they're actually being bought, as Facebook bought Instagram. They're paying jillions of dollars for companies that have never made a penny.

The critical thing is to take action and then get feedback. This is one quality of peak performers: they always take action and get feedback. The rule is, get an idea, take action, fail fast, learn quickly, try again. Complete the circle again. Repeat. Get an idea, try it out, get feedback, make a mistake, learn, and try it again. It's an endless cycle. Jim Collins calls it "the doom loop." Keep making mistakes, learning lessons and making mistakes, and finally it starts to move faster, and faster, and faster. Every successful person has made an enormous number of mistakes, as we said earlier. You start off with a direction, you take your first step, you start to move toward the goal, and you get feedback, and you use that feedback to change your course of action.

The same *Harvard Business Review* article mentioned another business that had made thirty-four changes in their business model before it hit. Drucker used to say four, but that was, I think, in the old days. Today it's ten or fifteen. One very successful business did ninety-nine tries, ninety-nine different iterations in the lean startup, although they were small. Try, learn, change. Try, learn, change. Try, learn, change. Because ego and learned helplessness and the comfort zone are all fighting against us, we often try something and, if it doesn't work, give up. "It must have been the wrong idea." No, try it again. Try it again. Try it again. Keep adjusting.

This is why flexibility is so important. You know that wonderful quote from Charles Darwin: "Survival goes not necessarily to the strongest or most intelligent of the species, but to the one most adaptable to change."

Back in the '90s a major institute in New York did a study, and they asked, what would be the most important quality for success in business in the twenty-first century? They looked at all of the qualities—vision, courage, ambition, persistence, innovation—but the number one quality is flexibility. Flexibility, the willingness to be flexible in the face of changing situations, changing circumstances. What is a good indication that you need to be flexible, that you need to adapt, that you need to change your course of action? The answer is, it's not working. You're not getting the results that you expected. So that just means back to the drawing boards.

Dan

So the fact that you have gotten a result that hasn't worked the first or second time is not necessarily a reason to be discouraged. It's a reason to learn, adjust, and act again.

I want to relate this idea of right action to the concept of adaptability and flexibility and why these two qualities are vital to success in today's world. That brings to mind the example of the bamboo tree. I've taken these seven principles from the website Presentation Zen. There are seven lessons from the Japanese forest, seven lessons from the bamboo tree, and what it can teach us about being flexible in today's modern world. I'm going to state each one for you and then have you extrapolate on that principle as it relates to an individual and his or her life.

The first of the seven is that *a bamboo tree bends, but it doesn't break.* It's flexible, yet it's firmly rooted. How would you translate that to an individual?

Brian

Harvard did a study among leaders, asking them about their biggest failures and how they coped with failure. They got blank looks from several hundred CEOs, who said, "Really, we've never failed in this company." "Yes, but you launched this product or this service, and it didn't work." They said, "No, no, those weren't failures. Those were just learning experiences. We never fail. We just learn things." Some of them were expensive learning experiences and difficult learning experiences and painful learning experiences, but leaders always look at a situation as a learning experience.

To go back to the bamboo tree, the roots are the absolutely unshakeable belief that you are going to be successful sooner or later, and that this is just a short-term setback. Whatever's happening to you, if it's not working out, that's fine. Take a deep breath, step back, and do something else.

Dan

So with all the change that goes around in our world, we have to be flexible. But we still need to have strong, rooted core principles.

Can you talk about the difference between compromising on a core principle, which is a timeless truth, and adapting to a situation? What is the difference between the two? In other words, you're not necessarily flexible on strong core principles. Would you agree?

Brian

The studies show that leaders are very clear about their values, and they never compromise them. I've written twenty books on management, and I've read probably 200 or 300—or 2000 or 3000—books over the years, and it always comes down to the same thing: integrity. Integrity means remaining consistent with the values that you agreed upon.

The entrepreneur Guy Kawasaki says that the first thing you do when you start a business is sit down with the key people and ask, "What do we believe in? What are our fundamental values? What are the unshakeable principles that we're going to work on?"

Usually the principles are very simple, and there are not more than three to five. They're things like absolute integrity, internally and externally; high-quality products that we stand behind; a commitment to customer service; a commitment to developing people; or having good results with people. In one great company I worked with, profitability was number five. We're not here in business to lose money, but the most important principle always comes first and dominates the next principles. The second principle dominates the lower principles. So you'll always organize your principles in sequence.

I remember talking to Tony Robbins about how your preeminent value takes precedence over all your others. Let us say your desire for success, to earn a lot of money, is very high, but your fear of failure and making a mistake is slightly higher. The most intense emotion will actually dominate the less intense emotion.

So pick your values. An example I sometimes use: imagine you meet two men at a party, and each of them has the same values. The first man's values are my family, my health, and my success. The second man has the same three values, but his are my success, my family, and my health.

Would there be a difference between these two people? Would there be a little difference or a big difference? There would be an enormous difference. A person who puts their family ahead of success or anything else is going to be a very different person from a person who puts success ahead of everything else.

I remember a friend I used to have. He was married, with children, a nice guy, very successful, very smart. I remember we were at his home, there were about six or eight of us there, couples, and we were talking about business. He said, "Well, I know one thing for sure. My financial success takes precedence over my family or anything else." And I remember looking at his wife. She had this flat, cold, shocked look on her face.

Before it was over, she had died of cancer, primarily caused by stress, the son was an alcoholic, the daughter had gotten pregnant and moved away, and the man ended up with a second wife and was broke. He moved to a small town in Arizona, where he lives to this day. Brilliant, bright, smart, but every single time push came to shove, the money came first, not the friendship, not the reputation, not anything else.

So it's really important to think about what your values are, and those are your roots. There are about fifty-four values that you can have, and a couple of my books have pages of the values you can pick from. But I've always told my kids that the two most important values are to accept responsibility and always tell the truth. If you have those two values, all the other values will fall into place naturally.

And my kids—I'm so proud of them: they're famous among their social circles for never lying or exaggerating. They always tell the truth. And they never blame anybody. They always accept responsibility.

They're happy, and popular, and successful, and living great lives. All around them are people who are alcoholic, and unemployed, and engaging in questionable activities, and taking dope. These kids are having a great time, because they're responsible and they always tell the truth.

Dan

Outstanding. The second quality of the bamboo tree is that *what looks weak is strong.* Bamboo doesn't look impressive, but it endures cold winters and extremely hot summers, and it will be the only tree left standing after a typhoon. How can you relate that idea to an individual being flexible in life?

Brian

In Jim Collins's wonderful book called *Good to Great,* he looked at companies that had been average for a long time and then became great companies, world leaders. He found that for each one of them, the turning point on the road to greatness was when they appointed what he called a "Level 5 leader." A Level 5 leader was not someone in the newspapers, in the press, or on the talk shows.

This person was usually very calm, easygoing, had a tremendous commitment to the success of the business, loved the business, and had very high moral values as well. These spread out through the entire company—quality people, quality relationships, quality customers, quality products, quality services, and this absolute determination and commitment to excellence.

Because of this, the whole company transformed. Some of them became some of the great companies of the world. In addition, according to the studies, these companies were the most flexible in any kind of economic situation. They always had cash reserves. They always were willing to change their strategy. They always were willing to pull back if the economy shrank. So they just kept going on and keep doing it. They keep going strong—big, highly respected, and profitable year after year.

Dan

I remember reading the same thing about the Level 5 leader. That's a perfect illustration of this idea of what looks weak is actually strong. But in the short term, the media tend to focus on the celebrity-like CEOs, the Mark Cubans of the world.

The ones that Jim Collins talked about were these men or women behind the scenes who, as you say, love the company. They're doing their work diligently day after day after day. They're not in the headlines. It's all about putting the company first over themselves. Because of that, and because they've built this foundation of success and trust within the organization, they are strong.

The third quality of the bamboo tree is *it's always ready*. Bamboo needs little processing or finishing. How would you relate that to an individual or a company?

Brian

I was just reading an article by Charlie Munger, who is Warren Buffett's right-hand man and a multibillionaire as a result, and who has been his friend all these years,. Charlie Munger said, "If you're not continually learning and growing in the world of today, you're not going to have a chance in the future."

Warren Buffett is the second or third richest man in the world. He'd be the richest if he hadn't given $22 billion to Bill Gates for his foundation. He started with nothing, built it up, and he spends 80% of his time every day reading. Carlos Slim, the fourth or fifth richest man in the world, also spends 80% of his time reading.

These people just read and read and read and learn. They fill their minds with new information and ideas on all the areas that are important to their business. As a result, they make brilliant decisions year after year. They buy into industries, or parts of industries, or buy out industries that nobody was looking at. It's always a front page story: Buffett buys this company or that company. It turned out that this company had hidden assets and a tremendous potential to be made far more profitable. Nobody else had seen it, but because of his reading, and his study, and his talking to people, he got those incredible insights.

So when you say, be always ready, it means be continually learning. You should be current with everything that's going on in your field. I have one seminar called the Two Day MBA, which is a crash course in practical business management. I have another seminar called Business Model Reinvention. It's also a two-day crash course. It covers twelve parts of a business model and gives a profit model for any business. It shows you that if your profits are down for any reason, it means that one of these parts or elements in the system is broken or obsolete. The market has changed. Whatever you were doing before to generate profits is not working, and the challenge is you're in a comfort zone.

I give people all of these ideas, and it's amazing: 80% of those people go back and transform their businesses. They say this is incredible stuff. But who is at these seminars? The best business people in every community. The top managers. The top entrepreneurs. The most successful people, whose time is really valuable. They're there, and they're in front, and they're taking notes, because they recognize that if they don't keep upgrading their skills with the most current information possible on business success, they're going to fall behind their competitors, who *are* keeping up with their skills.

Dan

Excellent. The fourth quality of the bamboo tree is *unleash your power to spring back.*

Brian

One of the most important qualities for success is resilience, which is exactly this—the ability to bounce back.

I teach this concept over and over—you are only as free as your well-developed options. In life, if you have only one choice, if there's only one job you can do, there's only one skill that you have, you're trapped. If something changes, if you lose a job, if your skill becomes obsolete, as they do, if your ability to produce a product becomes obsolete—many of these people go home, and you read about them. They don't work for two or three years. They sit at home and watch television, because their one skill is no longer in demand. The only way that you can develop more options is by keeping and developing new skills, learning more things. That will give you lots of flexibility and options and will give you the power to spring back.

Here's another thing that's really important: sleep. As it happens, in this last week I've been reading a book on brain functioning. It says that adequate sleep is absolutely essential for proper brain functioning.

Imagine charging your cell phone when the battery's in the red. Well, you need to recharge your mental battery as well. You see, everybody reading this is a knowledge worker. They don't work with their bodies, making and moving things. They work with their brains. The most important thing you can do is to keep your brain fully charged.

A recent study found that millionaires and billionaires sleep an average of eight and a half hours a night. Nonmillionaires sleep six or seven hours a night. The richest people get 8.46 hours. That's the number, and they get up before 6:00 a.m. That means they've got to go to bed by 9:00, so they can get their eight or eight and half hours of sleep.

When you do this, you have much more resilience. No matter what happens, you're calm and you're relaxed. You're not tired, or strung out, or irritable, or frustrated, or thinking about going back to bed. I joke with my audiences. I'll say, "How many people here this morning, when you got up the first thing you thought about was when you could go back to bed again tonight?" Fifty percent of the audience raise their hands. I say, "That means that you're not getting enough sleep." They're running with a sleep deficit.

And so I've said to my clients, "Go to bed at 9:00, turn everything off, shut down the television, and get eight, nine, even ten hours of sleep." And they come back, and they're transformed. They've got more energy. They've lost weight. Because if you're not getting enough sleep, you eat too much to try to compensate for that energy. You drink too much coffee, you take too many soft drinks, and at night you drink a whole bottle of wine. You're doing anything possible to get yourself pumped, because you're tired all the time.

As soon as they start getting eight and a half or nine hours sleep a night, they become more effective, they earn more money. Sometimes they triple their income in the first ninety days. They're healthier, they're much more personable with their families, their senses of humor are better, they make better business decisions, they're more influential and persuasive with others.

To unleash your power to spring back, get lots of rest. If you have lots of rest, you can endure almost anything that happens out there. But if you're tired and irritable, you're going to make short-term decisions. You're going to react and overreact, you're going to say things that you regret, and you're going to make decisions that are going to be very expensive to correct in the future.

Dan

That's fascinating, because I think you've just busted another myth. A lot of people think, "Millionaires and billionaires must have no time to sleep." That really flips this notion on its head.

Brian

One thing we teach in time management is that sometimes the best use of your time is to come home early, go to bed, and sleep the whole night. It's not to get caught up, to get more things done. Here's the other discovery: if you get lots of sleep, you become much more productive, you do much more work. You do better work, and you make fewer mistakes. What may take you eight hours to do if you're tired and you're dragging, you'll do in two or three hours, and it will be much better work. It's a great payoff. You don't lose. You actually gain time and productivity by being well rested.

Dan

The fifth principle is to *find wisdom in emptiness*. The hollow insides of bamboo reminds us that we are often too full of ideas and conclusions to embrace new knowledge. Can you expand upon that a little bit, this idea that emptying oneself can be helpful for an individual?

Brian

One of the great discoveries is the power of your intuition in guiding you unerringly to do and say the right thing. Emerson called this "the still, small voice within." However, in order to tap into your intuition and into what is called your superconscious mind, you have to create zones of silence.

I just finished a book on the different ways of using your time, and one of them was on mindfulness. Mindfulness is a very big subject right now. People are taking five-day retreats and paying thousands of dollars to learn how to be mindful. All you really have to do is go and sit in the silence.

A person begins to become great when they begin to listen to their inner voice. The way you listen to your inner voice is you turn off everything, put aside everything—no cigarette, magazine, music, anything—and go and sit quietly by yourself for at least thirty minutes. It's like a bucket of muddy water: your brain takes about twenty-four to twenty-six minutes to go clear.

Just go and sit for thirty to sixty minutes quietly. In the first thirty minutes, you'll have this irresistible impulse to get up and do something. Just stay there, and at the end of that thirty minutes, or even earlier, you'll suddenly become calm and clear, and your mind will start to become almost enlightened. Then the answer to the biggest problem that you're facing right now will just coast into your mind. It will be clear, like a great billboard. You just look up, and there's the answer. But this only works if you practice solitude on a regular basis.

Pascal, the great writer, once said that all the problems of the human race happen because of the inability of a man to sit quietly in a room by himself for any period of time. Instead of doing that, they get out and they start wars and revolutions and everything else.

But people who sit quietly and let their minds calm, and just think about themselves and their lives, are much calmer, much more creative. They make better decisions, they're much more personable, they have much lower flash points, they don't get angry very much. They smile a lot, and they just remain calm. Thus one of the most important things you can do if you want to be successful is to do nothing for thirty or sixty minutes each day.

Dan

I remember you talking about that at a seminar around twenty years ago, I remember hearing that very idea and doing that myself. This has so much more value even today, because it's almost as if silence has become a prized piece of gold. Everywhere you go, they have TVs, there's this noise pollution. Unless we are out in nature, or we intentionally silence ourselves, we can hardly hear that inner voice. Otherwise it's always being covered over.

The sixth principle of the bamboo tree is to *commit to continuous growth*. Bamboo trees are among the fastest growing plants in the world, so talk a little bit about this idea. It's like this idea of *kaizen*, if you will—the Japanese idea of continual improvement.

Brian

Zig Ziglar used to tell a great story about the Chinese bamboo tree. The farmers go out and they plant the bamboo trees. They put in the seeds, and they water, and they cultivate the bamboo trees, and nothing happens. They do this month after month. A year goes by and nothing happens. They do it again for the next year, and they keep doing this for five years and still nothing happens. What was happening was that the bamboo tree was developing a very, very deep root system. And then the bamboo tree grows 100 feet and becomes one of the strongest plants in the world. The only reason it can hold the 100 feet is that it has this deep root system.

It's the same thing with you when you are learning, and growing, and developing new knowledge and skills. Remember: one idea can change your life. But you never know what the idea is, so you must be continually taking in lots of new ideas, so that the right idea will come to you at the right time. It can transform your life completely.

I'll give you an example. I was listening to an interview with a successful entrepreneur. The interviewer said, "What's the key to being successful in business?" And the interviewee said, "Ninety percent of business success is determined by the quality of the product in the first place." I almost drove off the road when I heard that. I've seen this principle repeated a thousand times, but just the way it was phrased, that 90% of business success is determined by the quality of the product in the first place—that struck me.

I developed an entire two-day seminar around this: how do you organize, and plan, and develop, and sell, and market a truly excellent product? How do you know that it is *excellent*? What do you need to do? Where do you get the people, and the management, and the skills, and the techniques, and the customer service? You'll find that every successful company triggers this reaction from the customer: "This is a great product. Those are great people. This is a great place."

I ask my business owners, "How many people, what percentage of your customers, after using your product or service, turn to you or somebody else and say, 'Geez, this is a great product?' How many? Well, that percentage is the one single factor that determines your future in business. The percentage of people who say, 'This is a great product' determines your entire future." Millions of dollars have been spent on research on this subject. It's the one question: is this a great product?

People say, "Oh, I can understand that." And then I say, "But is it true for you as a person as well? Your success, your pay, your income, your promotion, your whole lifestyle will be determined by the quality of your work. And your job—and this comes from lots of research—is to get into the top 10% in your field. You don't have to be number one, like at the Olympics. You just have to be in the top 10%, because the top 10%, for both companies and individuals, earn 90% of the income that's distributed in any society. Just like the 80/20, this is a 90/10, so your job is to be in the top 10%."

What does it take to get into the top 10%? The answer is the decision to get there, because nobody can stop you from being in the top 10%. We're not talking about winning the Olympics. We're simply talking about being recognized as a high-quality producer or purveyor of your product or service.

Is it easy to get there? No. How long does it take? According to Malcolm Gladwell in *Outliers*, citing the work on elite performance, it takes five to seven years. In Jim Collins's *Good to Great*, the Level 5 leader, the really strong, quiet, calm, effective leader, took over five to seven years to make that company go from being a good company to being a world leader. So set that as your goal in your business life: "I want people to say that he's one of the best in the business." The doctors who are recognized as the top doctors earn $80,000, $100,000 a day. I know, because I use them, and I've got the bill from surgery. The average doctors are getting $150 a visit out in the suburbs.

They all went to the same medical schools, but the doctors—especially the surgeons—the ones who dedicated themselves to becoming really, really good at their craft, pulled ahead, like in a road race. They got further and further ahead of the average. Their income didn't go up by 10% or 20%. It went up by ten or twenty *times*. It all comes from continuous personal development, continually getting a little bit better every single day.

Dan

Finally, number seven: *express usefulness through simplicity.* The bamboo tree expresses its usefulness in its simplicity. Let's talk about this idea of simplicity and being useful in a simple way—that being successful really doesn't require enormous complexity.

Brian

There's been a lot of work done on the very popular subject of reengineering: how do you reengineer a business; how do you reengineer a personal life? The answer is to stop doing things. They looked at the strategies of major companies in this last recession. The ones who were successful were the ones who stopped doing the most things. Not the ones who started doing or trying the greatest number of new things—the ones who stopped doing things that weren't working that well.

So you have to ask, is there anything that I'm doing today that, knowing what I now know, I wouldn't get into again today? It seemed like a good idea at the time, and it probably was a good idea at that time, but knowing what I now know, I wouldn't get into it again. If the answer is "Yes, I would not get into this," the next question is, how do you get out and how fast? Don't delay, don't procrastinate. If you're in business and you decide that you have a person that you would not hire again today, let them go today. If you decide you have a product that you would not bring to the market again today because of competition, and price, and everything else, discontinue the product. Cut it off.

Often the senior executive who got the company into trouble is not capable of getting it out, because there's too much ego involvement in previous products and decisions. So what does the board of directors do? They bring in a turnaround artist. The turnaround artist has no emotional involvement. Usually, they're brought in for one year, maybe less, and they come in with a chainsaw.

One of the most famous turnaround artists was called "Chainsaw Dunlap." He could literally take a Fortune 500 company that was losing money and turn it around within twelve months. They'd give him a great big, fat bonus, and he'd walk off. There would be bodies everywhere. They'd bring in a new president, a democratic, authoritative president, and so on, and the company would restructure and become successful and profitable.

So I say, be your own turnaround artist. The key to success is to stop doing things. You cannot do more things than you're doing, so if you want to get control of your life, you have to stop doing things, which brings us to the reengineering process. The reengineering process is based on simply reducing the number of steps in each process. Andrew Grove wrote about this in *High Output Management* many years ago. He said, "Make a list of the steps in any process. Sit down very carefully and say, Step one, Step two. Maybe there are ten steps in a process. Then make a decision to eliminate 30% of the steps the first time through."

Then sit down with the people who are involved and ask, how can we eliminate these steps? Number one, you can eliminate it completely, because many steps have just gotten in there because of an emergency or a mistake. Number two, you can consolidate two steps or three steps together. Number three, you can discontinue that process, or that part of the process. Number four, you can outsource the process to another company that can do it better than you can. So there are several different ways to reduce the steps. The first time through, Andy Grove said, you've got to always shrink the number of steps by 30%. Then you go back again and say, "Let's do it again."

My favorite story was of Steve Jobs coming back into Apple in 1997. They gave him access to the books, and he found that the company was ninety days from insolvency, from closing its doors. They had thousands of people selling 104 products all over the world. He sat down and said, "We've got to stop the bleeding." He had every top executive come in and recommend ten products that they would continue with. All the others would be dropped.

People shouted and screamed and ran in circles, but they finally came in, because it was not a matter of choice. They came in with their ten, and they combined the ten together. They finally had a consensus. "Now," he said, "in the next few days I want you to go home, have discussions, and eliminate six more." Of course they were shocked. "It's either this or we close the company, so please understand your jobs are at stake here, and the jobs of thousands of other people."

They sulked and blustered, and some resigned, but they came back with four, and they cut 100 products. Out of 104 products they cut 100 products within ninety days. The whole company turned around. Within a few years it became the most valuable company in the world by stopping producing low growth, low income, low profit, no profit products. Get the ego completely out of the way. These products may have seemed like good ideas at the time, and there may be people that like them, but this company's got to survive. A most remarkable story.

So when you get overwhelmed in your life, sit down and say, "What do I need to stop doing?" And then start stopping it. Cut it off now.

Dan

You can relate this even to salespeople. Maybe you have clients, or you're going after clients, that are only going to give you a little bit in terms of sales or profitability. It's a matter of cutting them and keeping the most profitable 20%.

So, Brian, what's a final word that you want to give people about flexibility?

Brian

My great love, Peter Drucker, once said that errant assumptions lie at the root of all failures. In other words, wrong assumptions. We're assuming something that's not true; we're assuming there's a market that does not exist, or it's not big enough, or it's not profitable enough. We're assuming with a new product that there's a market for that. We're assuming that a person is going to turn around and become a good producer, when people never change. We're making the wrong assumptions.

The starting point is to question your assumptions and ask: what if I was wrong? What if my assumptions in this area, about the product, the service, the people, the market, the customers were completely wrong? What would I do then?

There are three or four questions that I teach in all of my business courses.

Number one is: what am I trying to do? Be clear. The answer is, you're trying to get business results. *Business results* mean that you're going to earn an excess of profits over all the costs involved.

Number two is: how am I trying to do it? You always ask this question when you're experiencing frustration, resistance, low performance, struggle, stress, anger, dissatisfaction with your work. Stop the clock and say, "What am I trying to do, and how am I trying to do it?" Very few people do that, but when they do, they think, "I'm trying to do it this way." And they say, "We must be kidding. We've tried to do it this way for five years, and it still hasn't worked."

Question number three is: is there a better way? Could there be a better way than the one we're using today? And the answer is there is always a better way. So, if we were not doing it this way now, knowing what we now know, would we start it this way again, or what would we do differently? You keep pushing it around, and that really keeps your mind open.

I'm going to be doing this with the senior executives of a $100 million company next week in Europe. We'll go around the table, and I'll ask these questions. These questions are like slapping people in the face. What are you trying to do? How are you trying to do it? Is it working? Why not? What are our assumptions? What if our assumptions were wrong, what would we do then? What if we had no limitations? What if we had an unlimited budget and we could do anything we wanted to do, and at the end of six months, if we hadn't accomplished the goal, they would come in and shoot us in the head, what would you do differently? What changes would you make immediately? Put the pressure on, and people start to come up with absolutely incredible ideas.

SIX

Sustaining Motivation, Part One: The Power of Daily Self-Talk

Dan

This is the first of three chapters in which we're going to talk about the importance of sustaining motivation through the process of any important accomplishment. Our tendency is to become stale, routine, and distracted. In the beginning you talked about all the modern distractions that we have from technology and elsewhere that take us off the route of our goals. And then there's just the fact that life passes by, and the years stack up upon one another, or people lose their focus.

Discuss how these next three chapters will give readers ideas, techniques, and strategies to overcome this common occurrence of losing their motivation.

Brian

We talked earlier about the power of suggestion in determining everything that happens to you. You're greatly influenced both by external influences and by internal influences. You can only respond and react effectively to external influences, but you need to take complete control of your internal influences, because they're far greater.

One thing that revolutionized my life was this very simple principle: that with affirmations, positive self-talk, your future and your potential are unlimited, because 95% of your emotions are determined by how you talk to yourself on an ongoing basis. You become what you think about most of the time. You also become what you say to yourself most of the time.

What are the words that you say to yourself? Remember that the default setting, the automatic setting, in the human brain is to talk to yourself in a negative way, to see the worst in things. This comes from childhood; maybe it's instinctive in human beings. You think about your worries and your pains and your grievances and your aggravations and your irritations, because these are the things that are the thorns in your side.

Very seldom do we deliberately choose to think about the things that we like and the things that make us happy. As you talk to yourself in a positive way, as you take control of this inner dialogue that's continually going night and day, even while you're asleep, you actually take control of your emotions. As you take control of your emotions, you take control of your attitude. You begin to change your beliefs as well, and you change your expectations.

The greatest single obstacle to success is the fear of failure, the fear of loss. What if I lose my job? What if I lose my money? What if I lose my time? What if I lose the love of someone else?

This is always manifested in the feeling *I can't. I can't change, I can't do this, I can't improve things.* It's learned helplessness. What is the antidote to this fear of failure? The answer is *I can do it.* Instead of saying *I can't* and becoming angry, you say *I can, I can do it, I can do anything I put my mind to.*

I learned this four decades ago, and I practice it on my children. I've told them from the very beginning, "When you grow up, you're going to be a big success." I program them with this. It's like sitting down next to their mental computers when they aren't watching. When they're young, children are susceptible; they have no ability to block the input of information from their parents. Whatever the parent says to the child repeatedly when the child is vulnerable becomes a permanent part of the child's makeup.

If the child is told over and over again how much their parents love them and how wonderful they are, and parents play with them and give them eye contact and hold them and walk with them and treat them like they're really important, this is what locks into their subconscious mind in the first three years of life. From then on, they build their whole life on that.

Fortunately, you can go back and reprogram an upbringing of negativity by repeating the words over and over again, *I like myself. I like myself. I like myself.* This drives the idea deeper, like pilings used to build a bridge. It drives it deeper into your subconscious mind and eventually cancels out any negative programming that you might have had.

The second thing that parents do when they're raising children is in order to protect them: they keep saying, *stop, get away from that, don't do that, don't touch that.* The child who is driven by its natural instincts to explore its environment only hears *I'm too small, I'm incompetent, I'm incapable, I can't.* At a very early age children stop trying new things, they stop exploring, because they know that their parents are going to get mad at them.

The child's greatest fear is the fear of loss of a parent's love. It's also true for adults. That's why the greatest gift of a parent is unconditional love, when they make it clear that they love their children 100%, no matter what they do or say, and they back them 100%.

I had an experience with this unconditional love. I once got an emergency call from the country club. My son and his friend, who were about ten or eleven years old, had gone over there, and they were playing around. They got some shampoo from the locker room. They took it with them, and they put it in the Jacuzzi outside.

Well, it frothed up, and people came running. The management came out, and they called the police. Then they called us. We drove over there. There were two police cruisers, there were the people from the country club, and you'd think there'd been a massive robbery. But it was just this Jacuzzi foaming up.

My son David and his friend were petrified. I asked the police, "What's happening?" They said, "Well, kids are just kids, they got a big scare. Country club's making too much of this. We have to stand by like there's a serious crime in progress." I said, "Thank you, don't worry, I'll take them home."

I took Michael home, put him in the back seat, drove him home, never said a word. When we got home, I said, "What happened?" "Well, we just got the shampoo." I said, "Sheesh, we did dumber things than that when we were young. That's OK. Go to bed now."

Two days later the country club phoned us up and kicked us out. They canceled our membership because of our juvenile delinquent children. I went to David said, "David, you got us kicked out of the country club." His eyes lit up, and I said, "But it's OK, don't worry, it doesn't matter." He was clear that he was safe.

I took David to Europe with me two weeks ago. We were talking about how I've always given him unconditional love. He's twenty-nine years old now, and he said, "I remember the country club. I remember when you came and picked me up. You took me home, and you never said a word. You backed me 100%. I still remember that. You did that with all of us; it was the greatest thing in the world."

Anyway, my point is this continuous flow of positive verbal messages to your children, and to your spouse, to your grandchildren, and to other people. Constant positive reinforcing is one of the most wonderful things you can do. Positively reinforce yourself as well.

There's another law that says that whatever is *expressed* is *impressed*. Whenever you say anything that raises the self-esteem and self-confidence of another person, you automatically raise your own self-esteem and self-confidence. By making another person feel happy and positive, you feel happy and positive.

If you are going to take a first-aid course, when do you take it? At the scene of the accident, when somebody is bleeding, or before? Obviously you want to take it before so that you're fully prepared.

It's the exactly same thing with positive self-talk and reversals and setbacks in life. Talk to yourself on a positive basis all the time, so that when you experience the unexpected reversals and failures, you are subconsciously prepared to be resilient, like the bamboo tree. You will take the initial shock, and you will bounce back immediately.

Talk to yourself and say these magic words: *I can do it. I can do it. I can do it.* If somebody else is doubtful say, *you can do it.* Many people's lives have been changed by one person saying *you can do it.* You have incredible ability.

Whenever I'm out anywhere and I meet anyone who is doing a good job, especially in waitressing, or in business, or hotels, I say, "You know, you're going to be a big success sooner or later. You've got star quality, and you're going to be a big success." I may never see them again, but I know that many people's lives were changed forever by one person taking the time to tell them that they were good and that they had great potential.

After all the negative messages in their lives, they grab onto your message, and they hold that message. I've had people come up to me and say, "You may not remember, but I was in jail and you wrote to me," or "I met you at a seminar in Kansas City, and my life was in shambles. Now this is my life today, and it's wonderful. I have my own business, a beautiful home, and family, and everything else. You changed my life. You took the time to talk to me, you wrote to me, you called me, you sent me a message. I still have it, I still look at it, I have it on my desk, because nobody had ever told me that."

This law of reversibility says that the more you tell other people how good they are, the more you say the same things to yourself. Also, the more you talk to yourself in a positive way, the more naturally you talk to other people in a positive way.

Dan

Excellent. Brian, is there any kind of formal process that you recommend, like the one you have with goals, when it comes to creating a habit of positive self-talk? It's for people who think, "Consciously, when I force myself to say these positive things, I can say them, but then I have this ongoing chatter. I'm so used to putting myself down." Is there a process you recommend for people to get in the habit of positive self-talk day after day?

Brian

Yes, there is a process. Napoleon Hill called it *autosuggestion*. Auto-suggestion means self-suggestion, which goes back to our talk about the power of suggestion. Today we call it *autoconditioning*: we are conditioned by ourselves.

There are two types of conditioning. One is autoconditioning, where you condition yourself by talking to yourself. Then there's *heteroconditioning*, which means being conditioned by others, by having them talk to us and influence us. The best, of course, is to have both, but at least you can control autosuggestion.

There's a five-step process that you can use to learn how to talk to yourself in a positive way. The first step of the process is to *idealize*. Idealize means that you project yourself forward, you use the magic wand theory, and you imagine that your life is perfect in every way. If your life were perfect in every way, what would it look like? What would you be doing? How would you feel? What would you be accomplishing?

I teach this to corporations who are going through strategic planning exercises. I'll have everyone in the room imagine that this company is perfect in five years. If it were perfect in five years, how would people describe it from the outside? If a major magazine were going to do a story on this company, and they fanned out and they interviewed everybody connected with this company—customers and suppliers and vendors and competitors and staff—what would you want them to say?

People around the table say things like, "This is the best company in its industry," with the highest-quality products, great customer service, tremendous technology, regular growth rates, stock value three times as high as it was five years before, the best leadership, the best training, the best people, and so on. (These, by the way, turn out to be the characteristics of all the best companies.) I say, "All right, now, are these ideals possible?" They all say stop and they say, "Yes. Not in one year, but in three years or five years, we could accomplish all of those."

I walked a company through this process a few years ago. They came up with seventeen ideal descriptions, almost like affirmations of what the company would look like if it was perfect in five years. At that time they were at $20 million in sales. One of their goals was to be at $40 million, with double the sales and of course double the profitability.

They began to initiate all of these ideas enthusiastically; everyone got into it. Five years later, they called me and invited me to a special dinner in downtown Washington at the Ritz Carlton: "We'd like you to come; we're celebrating our five-year anniversary of that strategic planning session." They paid for my way and everything else, so I went.

It was beautiful. They had a live jazz orchestra, fabulous food, everything. Then they got up and they made the announcements. The announcement was that this year they had hit $104 million in sales, five years after they had set a goal to hit $40 million. In other words, they exceeded their goal by 500%, and they said it was all because of that exercise in idealizing.

The first thing you do to exceed your goals is to create an exciting future picture of what your business and your life would look like sometime in the future if they were perfect in every way. The second thing you do is you *visualize*. You imagine; you create a mental picture of that success. Remember, you cannot accomplish something on the outside unless you can visualize it and see it on the inside.

One couple went through this seminar explaining this process about idealizing and visualizing. They said they wanted to have a dream house. I said, "Then get some pictures of dream houses. Buy some beautiful magazines that are full of pictures, like *House Beautiful* and *Architectural Digest* and *Better Homes and Gardens*."

They went out and did that. Two years passed. It was the most amazing story. They called me up and said, "You're not going to believe what happened after that seminar. We went out and we idealized. We found these magazines and we subscribed to them, and we started to tear out pictures of rooms and gardens so that we could create our perfect composite home.

"Then we made a big file folder with all these pictures. We would take it out, and we'd look at it every week. We'd think about and dream about living in that home. Then, a year later, we got an announcement that my husband was being transferred out west." In this case it was to Edmonton, Alberta.

The first thing the husband had to do was buy a house. He went out on a Tuesday or Wednesday. He called up a couple of real estate agents, and he remembered this picture, this dream that he had. He said, "We're looking for a house that has these aspects and this view and this number of rooms." The listing agent said, "Well, I know everything in the inventory in town. There is no house like that for sale right now, but there is a house just like that coming on list tomorrow. You could be one of the first people to see it."

His wife came out on Friday, and Saturday morning the real estate agent picked them up from the hotel. They drove out to this house, and they walked in. It was the perfect house from *Better Homes and Gardens*–the one that they had been dreaming about and visualizing for two years. The price was right, the location was right. They bought the house, and they're living in it today. They said, "It was like a dream; it was the house we had dreamed of."

Visualizing is really important, and here are the rules. There are five parts to visualization. The first is *clarity*. The greater clarity you have of the mental picture of the person you want to be, or the things you want to have, the faster they come into reality. It's almost like a one-to-one relationship: clarity and realization.

Number two is *vividness*. How vivid is the picture that you see? Number three is *intensity*: how excited are you about achieving this goal? The next is *duration*: how long can you hold this visual picture in your mind before being distracted? The fifth, final principle is *repetition*: how often each day do you create this mental picture?

These five factors of visualization are never explained anywhere. Not even in *The Secret* or any of these other books, because these people have not done their research. This research comes from India, with those five principles: clarity, vividness, intensity, duration, repetition. Step number three is to *verbalize*. Remember, your mind is activated by powerful words; this is where you create an affirmation. You can say, "I live in a beautiful 5000-square-foot home overlooking the river valley, in a lovely neighborhood, where my children can go to excellent schools." That's a good verbalization. It's maybe a bit long, but now you have a clear picture. If you're not specific in your verbalization, there may be a house for sale, but it might not have a view. There's a house for sale, but it might not be in a good neighborhood. There's a house for sale, but it's too small or too large.

In other words, the universe wants you to be crystal clear about what you want. It's like planting a seed in a very rich soil. The universe, nature, will grow the seed. Your job is to plant it and keep it clear: keep the weeds away. Nature will just grow it naturally.

If you don't plant flowers in a garden, what will grow? Weeds. Weeds—negative thinking—grow automatically. With flowers, vegetables—positive thinking—you have to weed them. Verbalize and create a clear verbal statement of your goal.

For many years, I got three by five index cards, and I would write my affirmations: *I achieve this goal by this date. I weigh this amount. I swim this far. I drive this type of a car. I live in this type of a home. I earn this amount of money.* I never wrote anything on those cards that I didn't eventually achieve: be a best-selling author, travel around the world, earn a certain amount of money, live in a beautiful home, have lovely children. I wrote everything down and reread it over and over. One of the most powerful forms of affirmation is written affirmation. You write down your positive statements in words, and then you reread them and you recite them to yourself every day.

I would also review my affirmations morning and night. You can work on as many as fifteen goals at a time this way. Every morning I would sit and read the goal, and I would create a picture of this goal as already achieved. The next step is you emotionalize. You think how you would feel if you achieved this goal—proud, happy, excited, warm, thrilled, secure, whatever it happens to be. Combine the emotion with the verbalization.

I earn this amount of money by this date. If I earn this amount of money, how will I feel? What will I do, what will I look like, what will be different in my life? You've got to make that affirmation come to life. It's got to be vivid, exciting, clear, emotional, and intense. It's got to be written so that you can trigger the picture and the emotion every time you read it. I would read it twice a day and take a few seconds and visualize the goal as already realized.

The next step is to *actualize*—in other words, take the actions consistent with achieving the goal. Act as if the goal is guaranteed, and do the actions that come to your mind; do the actions that lie clearly at hand. Get up each morning, go to work, do the very best job you can, and have absolute trust that the goal is moving towards you in the most remarkable ways.

The final principle is called *realization*. At exactly the right time for you, in exactly the right way, the goal will appear. It will appear not too soon and not too late; you can never push to have the goal appear. The goal will appear exactly when you are ready for it, so just be patient and completely trusting, as though an extremely wealthy man of high integrity had absolutely guaranteed that he was going to deliver this goal to you at exactly the moment that was best for you. Just relax, as though it's money in the bank.

This relaxation creates the catalyst. It's almost like the chemical substance within which the goal is realized. The more relaxed you are, the more calm you are, the more rapidly the goal materializes in your life.

As you see, I've studied the principles of self-talk, autosuggestion, autonomic conditioning, and so on. These are all the things that you need to do, and if you do them, you'll find your whole life starts to dance. You're more positive, you have more energy, and stuff starts to happen around you. It's all consistent with moving you towards the goal.

Dan

That's great advice, especially for people who are feeling stale or as if they've gone off the path. Putting those steps into practice on a daily basis would be a huge help to sustaining the motivation that they need.

One thing that's related to self-talk is the idea of questions. We're always either talking to ourselves or we're asking questions of ourselves. We're either asking positive questions like, *how can I do this?* and *how can I solve this?* or negative things like, *why does this always happen to me? Why am I a person who can never follow through?*

We are all asking ourselves questions every day. Again, it seems that the negative approach is the most common. *Why does that always happen to me? Why can't I afford what I need?* are probably two very common questions in our country today. Rather than empowering questions, such as *what can I do to afford what I need?*

Can you discuss how to craft empowering questions to help people motivate themselves?

Brian

In Martin Seligman's research at the University of Pennsylvania, they interviewed 350,000 people over a twenty-two-year period. One question they asked was, "What are you thinking about most of the time?" The answer that came back was that top people think about what they want and how to get it most of the time.

The most important question in continuous motivation is to think about what you want, and think what actions you can take now to move you closer to the goal. How can I achieve this goal? Every time you ask the question *how*, you trigger action ideas, things that you can do immediately to take one step towards the goal.

Napoleon Hill said, "The only real cure for worry is continuous action in the direction of your goals, because you get so busy working towards your goals, you have no time to think negatively at all." The rule is never say anything that you don't want to be true about yourself.

Don't say, "I always mess up," or "Why do I make mistakes like this?" Always say, "What can I learn from this that will make me smarter next time?" Your mind can only hold one thought at a time. If you ask this question, and you focus on your lessons—what did I learn from this?—you don't have time to be negative at all, because looking for a positive lesson makes you a positive person. It makes you happy, it gives you energy.

Here's the discovery again. You will always find at least one, and sometimes several, lessons that you can learn from any setback or difficulty. All, or almost all, wealthy people today have made an enormous number of mistakes on the way to wealth. They've learned from each mistake. Unsuccessful people make a mistake, and they blame it on others. Successful people make a mistake, and they look upon it as a gift from God: "There's something in this that can help me to make sure that I am fully prepared when I do achieve my success."

Again, quoting Earl Nightingale: "If you achieve your success and you're not ready for it, you'll just feel foolish, and you'll lose it quite quickly." Easy come, easy go. The way to hold onto your success, when it inevitably comes, is to learn from every experience. They say that wisdom is making the same mistake over and over again, and recognizing it. Well, wisdom is really not making the same mistake over again. You ask, "What did I do right, and what would I do differently in this experience if I had to do it over?"

What you would do differently contains all the lessons learned in the experience. You can stomp on the accelerator of your self-growth, your personal learning, by constantly reviewing your performance, but in a positive way.

Dan

Excellent. I was reading that when you actually learn something and believe it, and then teach it to other people, you instill it in yourself at a deeper level. Just teaching what you're trying to master to someone else has such a powerful effect.

Can you talk about why that is? That when there's something you're trying to master yourself, when you take the role of the teacher, it has such a powerful impact in terms of your own learning and mastery?

Brian

You become what you think about, you become what you talk about to yourself, and you become what you teach. If we have a compulsion to teach, it's because we want to learn the subject ourselves at a deeper level. That's why you become what you teach.

In order to teach something, you have to really go into the subject in depth. You have to look at it from many different sides. Once you have learned the subject, you lose interest in teaching it. You'll want to teach other things.

I teach business model reinvention. I put in 300 hours of studying over two years. I read all the best books and articles on the subject, and took notebooks full of notes, and then reviewed the notes. Then I put together workbooks, and I taught the subject. Then I revised the workbooks and taught it again, and revised and revised. I'm in my fifth and sixth revisions now.

I teach it in such a way that it really makes people happy; it gives them tools that they can use to be successful. I'm learning the same things myself, and I'm able to apply this idea of business model reinvention to my own business. My income has gone up, and my life satisfaction has also gone up.

Many years ago I took a course in accelerated learning. One part is called *dual-plane learning*. It was basically about how you can learn faster and retain longer. One thing they say is first, learn it yourself, but as you're learning it, think about teaching it.

You're actually taking in the information on two levels. You're having the information come in, and you're thinking about how you would teach this to someone else so they could get the same impact. If you're thinking about the information on two levels at the same time, that doubles and triples the amount that you learn and retain. You're much more likely to internalize the information if you think, "How could I teach this? To whom would I teach this? To whom would this be of value? What if I was going to write an article on this?"

When you're thinking about it like this, you learn at a much more rapid rate. When you start to actually teach it to people, your learning goes up five or ten times.

Dan

Brian, you told the story about your son and unconditional love, which was so powerful. This idea of self-talk is critical for a parent raising kids.

I've seen this in my own sons when they play sports. If they make a mistake or something bad happens, they'll hear the boos in the crowd. They'll come back down in the dumps. You can almost see the invisible thoughts of negativity swirling in their heads.

As a parent, how do you advise people to help their kids to start on a good note with self-talk? Obviously if they start young, they're going to be way ahead of the game than if they have to work on this as an adult.

Brian

Let's go back to this simple statement: *I like myself, I like myself.* I had a woman come up to me recently. She said she had heard that from me, and she struggled with it because of her negative upbringing. She didn't like herself, she didn't think she was that good, she felt inferior. Suddenly she had a breakthrough and she started saying to herself, *I love myself. I love myself.* She said that all she wanted as a child was for her parents to love her. Since her parents didn't love her, someone had to love her, and it had to be herself.

When your children doubt themselves, tell them, "You did a great job, you did the best you possibly could. You'll do better next time; there's always a next time." Tell them how good they are and how excellent they are.

One interesting study says that our self-esteem is largely created by the distance between our self-image, the way we see ourselves today, and where we dream of being in the future. It's also determined by where we are today relative to our expectations. Where did we expect to be at this stage at our life, and are we at that stage?

It's absolutely amazing how much depression, and alcoholism, and negative physical behavior is caused by people who've reached a certain stage in life. They expected to be much further along at that point, and they're not. They expected to have more money, more success, more income. This gap between where they expected to be and where they are causes them enormous stress. Sometimes they even kill themselves.

The highest rate of suicide in America is in males between the ages of forty-eight and fifty-two, because that's the point where they realize, *I'm never going to make it.* Which is not necessarily true, but they had such high expectations for themselves. This goes back to their parents. Their parents always demanded that they be excellent, always demanded that they win, always demanded that they excel.

I remember this story: this boy is going to school and he comes home with average grades. His father beats him up and breaks him. "Why are you getting such lousy grades? What's the matter, are you stupid or something?" The father beats him up, so the kid decides he's going to work hard and get good grades.

He cancels all of his social activities with his friends. He comes home, studies three, four, five hours a night for the entire semester. He takes six courses. Of the six courses, he's gotten five A's and one B, and he comes home and he shows his report card to his father. The father takes one glance at the report card and says, "Why did you get a B?" He said he never tried in school again; that just took away all the desire to excel. When he was thirty-five years old, he was still working in an average job. He said his father had destroyed his motivation, his incentive, with that behavior.

The most wonderful thing you can do is always tell your kids how good they are. "Hey, you did great, and you'll do better next time." Never be disappointed in your kids. Never go into it saying,

"If you'd only done this," or "if you had only done that differently," and so on.

It's like that story of my son with the soap in the Jacuzzi. I said, "That's OK, geez, I made those kind of mistakes when I was young." That's a formative event: twenty years later, he still remembers. He remembers how concerned he was with how I would respond to the police and everyone else, and I just laughed. We just laughed, and we've done that with every problem our kids have gotten into. All good kids get into stuff; we just laugh.

To come back full circle, you become what you say to yourself most of the time. You have total control over what you say to yourself most of the time. Deliberately talk to yourself in a positive way. Never say anything about yourself that you don't want to be true.

Never say, "Geez, I look overweight." You say, "My ideal weight is such and such, by such and such a date." Or "I weigh this number of pounds by this date." Always think about the future. Forget about the past, which you can't change. Always create affirmations for your wonderful exciting future, and those affirmations will come true just as surely as seeds bloom in summertime.

SEVEN

Sustaining Motivation, Part Two: Developing a Long-Term Perspective

Dan

Brian, now we're going to talk about a topic I know is very near and dear to your heart. I remember in the '80s particularly, people in the United States were worried about Japan as a real competitor to the U.S. Businesspeople in America were trying to emulate the Japanese focus on long-term planning and long-term thinking.

As the years have gone by and society has changed, we're now faced with electronic gadgets around us all the time—email and social media and all these distractions. It seems that there's an addiction to short-term results, short-term thinking, that's infected our society. So talk about how this addiction to short-term thinking and short-term results can be lethal to maintaining our motivation.

Brian

I call this the *expediency factor* or the *E-factor,* and I've done forty years of research on it. It basically says that the natural tendency of human beings is to look for the fastest and easiest way to get the things they want right now, with very little concern over the long-term consequences.

There are also two views of politics. One view says that everybody can be perfected, that human nature can be changed, that the lion can lie down with the lamb; it's just simply a matter of the best use of government policies and money. The other, the more conservative way, of looking at human nature is that human nature is immutable. It's fixed; it doesn't go away, and it doesn't change. It's the same for all human beings everywhere at all times, throughout all of human history.

So what is the purpose of good government? Good government is to create a structure of incentives such that people seeking their own best interests in the fastest way possible do something or produce something of use or value to other people.

The greatness of America was founded on *The Wealth of Nations* by Adam Smith, and Adam Smith says that people do not produce things for the good of other people. They do it for themselves. They know that if they produce very good quality products and they aggressively market and sell them, and these products improve the lives of others, it will, by extension, improve their own lives. That's free market economics. Free market economics says that everybody should be free to do anything they want to serve other people in order to serve themselves.

At Harvard University in the '50s, Dr. Edward Banfield completed a series of studies looking for the reasons for upward socioeconomic mobility—in other words, increasing income over time. He studied both nationally and internationally to find out why some people move up more rapidly in the income ladder.

He found that there are seven different socioeconomic levels. We call them classes, even though you're not supposed to talk about classes. In most countries, the classes are grouped like a triangle, with the masses at the bottom, a few people doing well above that, and then the elite, the rich, at the top.

America was the first society in the world designed as a diamond. At the bottom of the diamond, the lowest 5%, you have what is called the *lower-lower class*. These are people who cannot provide for themselves.

They are welfare cases. They may be alcoholic. They may have mental problems. They may live on the street, they may be homeless. It is astonishing how much public policy is aimed at dealing with and taking care of those people. Which is fine; it's what a prosperous society can do.

The second level is called *upper-lower class*. These are people who work as dishwashers. They work as street sweepers. They are new immigrants. They are people with limited education. People that work at McDonald's and places like that. They get their first job; they get their first foot on the ladder of income.

But they don't stay there, because the next level up is *lower-middle class*. Lower-middle class is where people work at jobs that require a certain amount of skill. You go from being a counter person at McDonald's to being a french fry maker or a supervisor or a hamburger maker. In other words, as you develop more skills, you become more valuable, you're paid more money, and you move up.

Then you go from the lower-middle class to the *middle-middle class*. These are the white-collar service workers. They're the predominant population of workers in our society. Everybody who works at an office or who delivers things and takes notes and uses a computer, and so on, is considered middle-middle class. In America, the middle-middle class is huge. It's maybe 60% of our population. The lower-lower class is only 5%, and the upper-lower class, maybe 10%, and so on.

Above the middle-middle class is the *upper-middle class.* The upper-middle class includes people with skills, like doctors, lawyers, architects, engineers. They have university degrees that qualify them to be in the professional class. These people, of course, earn far more money than people in the middle-middle class.

Above the upper-middle class is the *lower-upper class.* The lower-upper class consists of people who are first-generation wealthy. It's a person who becomes a millionaire or more in the first generation of work. Above that is *upper-upper class,* second or third generation money. These people have money that was made by their parents or their grandparents.

The upper-upper class, the wealthy people in our society, are never more than about 1%. In spite of all the political posturing about taxing these people, there are very few of them. Because they're so wealthy, they get into newspapers and magazines, and they do television specials on them, and so on.

Here's what Banfield found: there is only one quality that predicted rapid upper socioeconomic mobility, and that was long-time perspective. Long-time perspective meant that the individual spent a lot of time thinking in the long term—five and ten and even twenty years out into the future when planning their current activities. There was a great book called *Competing for the Future* in the '90s. It was about corporations, but it made the observation that long-term perspective dramatically improved short-term decisionmaking.

So one key to great success is to think in terms of where you want to be in the future—psychologically, financially, economically, socially—and then come back to the present, and ask, "What things do I have to do today to be sure that I achieve those goals in the long term?" This requires planning, thinking, sacrifice, hard work, delayed gratification.

The simplest way to become wealthy is to work hard and save your money and let it grow by compounding. When I started off in this field, there were something like 1 million self-made millionaires back in 1980. Today, there are 10 million self-made millionaires in the year 2016, and the number's growing by several hundred thousand each year.

Why is that? In 1980, I discovered that if you were to save $100 a month, $25 a week out of your income, and invest it carefully in a good mutual fund and let it grow with the rate of the economy, by the time you retired, forty-five years later, with compounding you'd be more than a millionaire. That's long-term perspective.

I've met farmers and crane operators and doormen and taxi drivers and laborers who became millionaires over the course of their working lives. The families on either side of them living in small houses were spending everything they earned and a little bit more besides on credit cards, while these people were saving 10%, 15%, 20% of their income and just tightening their belt a little bit. They were going out for dinner a little bit less, shopping at Walmart and buying products and paying a little less. They were looking for ways to cut corners, and then put the money away and never touched it.

So long-term perspective turns out to be the single most important quality for success. You could turn every single person in every single neighborhood in America into a highly paid person, but if they didn't have long-term perspective, they'd soon blow through all the money.

There is the 80/20 rule: the top 20% of people in a society have 80% of the wealth. You could take all the wealth of society and divide it up equally so that every single person starts with exactly the same amount, and within one year, the top 20% would have 80% of the money, because the top 20% are always looking for ways to create the future: to save, invest, and so on. The bottom 80% would just go out and blow it, and the top 20% would get it.

This is one of the most important things that I've ever discovered, and it's life changing. So ask yourself, what are your goals in ten or twenty years? Then every minute of every day ask yourself, "Is what I'm doing right now moving me toward my most important goals or not?"

Earlier I said I'd give you lots of ways to double your productivity. Here's a very simple technique, which I teach people, and they just shake their heads because it's so simple. Imagine that every day, you have tasks, and we'll call these A tasks and B tasks. A tasks are tasks and activities that move you toward the goals that you want to achieve. B tasks are activities that do *not* move you toward the goals that you want to achieve, or, even worse, they move you away from those goals.

So here's a wonderful way to double your productivity, to become rich, healthy, successful, and highly respected for the rest of your life: be crystal clear about your goals, and then do only A tasks all day long. Do not do B tasks at all.

That alone will supercharge your productivity. It will earn you the esteem and respect of everybody around you. It'll make you the go-to person in your field. It'll move you into the top 10% of your field in terms of the quality of your work. It transforms everything.

Just do A activities. These are the ones that have long-term consequences. They are the ones that contribute to your achieving the most important things in life.

So the most important part of developing a long-term perspective is to realize that it is the one predominant quality shared by all wealthy people.

Dan

This also applies to raising our children and the idea of delaying gratification. The classic example of this was the marshmallow test. A child is presented with a marshmallow and given a choice: eat this one now or wait to enjoy two later. What will the child do? Talk a little bit about the marshmallow test and its implications for that child's behavior later in life.

Brian

The marshmallow test was a great study. It was done at Harvard by a psychologist thirty or forty years ago, and I read about it at the beginning of my speaking career. They put a bunch of children, ages six to eight, in a room around a table, and they say, "Here is a marshmallow. We'll leave you here for half an hour. If you can refrain from eating this marshmallow for those thirty minutes, you'll get two marshmallows."

Then the researchers go out of the room and watch what they do through a one-way mirror.

Some kids sit and stare at the marshmallow; other kids put their hands over their eyes and look away from the marshmallow. Other kids put their arms under their shoulders and hold onto their arms to hold themselves back from touching the marshmallow. Still other kids pick up the marshmallow, put it down, and nibble at it, Then they put it down and eat a little bit more, and finally consume the whole thing.

Ten years later, they found that when these children were in their teens, the ones that had resisted eating the marshmallow were getting better grades. As they went into their twenties, they became high achievers. Even twenty years later, they were earning more money; they were in higher, senior positions.

As for the kids who had consumed the marshmallow immediately, nothing ever came of them. They got poor grades, they were not particularly successful or particularly popular, and ten or twenty years later, they were working at average jobs.

This brings us to a great question. What caused the difference in this behavior at an early age? Here's the answer. The kids who did not eat the marshmallows were brought up by their parents to feel confident and secure in themselves.

You see, the reason people eat a lot of food goes right back to prehistory, when you would be coming into the winter. In the wintertime, there would be no food, so you would eat a lot of food, like a bear that's going to hibernate. You'd eat, and you'd fatten up, because the lean months are coming.

So today, if a person is insecure and they get a chance to eat some food, to drink some liquor, to enjoy immediate gratification, they lurch for it, because in the back of their mind, they're not sure if they're going to get more in the future. They're not sure if they are going to be safe.

That's why, in dieting, if you starve yourself, when you start to eat again, your body puts on an enormous amount of weight because it has this idea registered: "Gee, I'd better load up here."

What do most overweight people do? When they go on a diet, all they think about is, "As soon as I lose five pounds, I can go out and gorge. I can go to the nearest restaurant, and I can pork out." Their reward for losing weight is to gorge. But if they starve themselves, their body says, *red alert, red alert,* and it they drives them to think about nothing but going out and gorging and repacking the food.

So if you are secure in yourself because your parents have raised you to feel like a valuable and important person, to feel that you're totally secure in their love, because they'd never take it away from you—we call this unconditional love—then these kids will pass the marshmallow test. It's not genetic. It's upbringing.

These kids are more successful in their teens and twenties. Why? It's because they grew up with high self-confidence and high self-esteem. When you have high self-esteem, you set bigger goals for yourself. You persist longer, and you become unstoppable. You just keep going and going, like the Energizer Bunny. It all goes back to those early childhood experiences.

Dan

Maybe you're somebody who wasn't raised that way. You didn't have that secure upbringing; you tend to give in to urges. It's something that you know deep down. What can you do today? What things can you surround yourself with, what habits can you implement, to help you act in this long-term manner of delaying gratification?

Brian

Psychology has developed some very powerful techniques to teach people to delay gratification. Goethe said, "Everything is hard before it is easy." One of the most important things is to develop good habits that enable you to be more happy and successful in life.

Interestingly, developing a good habit requires self-discipline, and self-discipline is very closely tied to self-esteem. Also, self-discipline is the single most important quality for success in life. So if you discipline yourself to hold off gratification, to complete a task before you give yourself a reward, that discipline will raise your self-esteem and self-confidence. It gives you a higher and better character. It makes you stronger, and every act of self-discipline strengthens every subsequent act of self-discipline.

So one thing you can do at the beginning is set up a reward system for task completion. A good friend of mine told me many years ago that when he got into sales, he had to sit there and phone to make appointments. He called it "dialing for dollars." I spoke to a Wall Street trader just last week, one of my clients, and he said there's a direct relationship between dials and dollars. It's just a matter of the dials—how many times you pick up the phone and dial. However, the fear of rejection holds people back tremendously. So my friend developed a very simple technique. He would take a steaming hot cup of coffee, and he'd put it in front of him all ready to drink. He said he would not give himself a sip of the coffee until he had made a first call and made contact with a prospect. Then he sat down with the phone, and he'd make the call, and he talked to the prospect and hung up the phone and gave himself a sip of coffee.

But the coffee was getting cold, so he'd make another call as quickly as he could, and he wouldn't care too much about whether or not the customer was interested. What he was concerned about was getting to the next sip before the coffee got cold. This is a form of inverted psychology, where you take your focus off the task and onto something different so that the stress of the task is diminished. He would do this. Each time he got through to somebody, he'd give himself a sip of coffee. By the time he got to the fifth person, the coffee cup was empty.

Then he came up with another idea. He liked cookies, but you don't want to be eating a lot of cookies. So he would take a cookie, and he would cut it into pieces, maybe half an inch by half an inch, in the way you would to reward an animal for performing an act.. Then he would give himself one little piece of cookie every time he made a call.

His friends would joke with him and say, "Look at this guy. He's doing all these games; he's playing with his head." Within three months, he was the highest earning salesman in this company. He was breaking every record, because he had more prospects. He would say, "I need ten prospects for this week," and he would just sit there and give himself a sip of coffee or a piece of cookie.

What happens is your mind starts to think more and more about the reward and less and less about the stress and tension of making the call and being rejected. So this is one thing you can do: set up a reward structure for engaging in a good behavior. For example, if you're doing a big job, divide it into small pieces, and give yourself a little reward for the completion of each small piece.

Maybe the first reward is a piece of cookie. Maybe you say that if do ten calls, you give yourself a stand up and stretch and a walk around and a chat with someone else. Maybe if you make twenty calls, you check your email for the first time in the day.

Remember, checking emails is a dessert activity; it's not a dinner activity, and the key to success is to have dinner before dessert. The logical place for dessert is not first. Checking email is dessert, so if you come in in the morning and you check email, you're eating your dessert first.

It's exactly the same as if you sat down at dinner at night and you had a whopping big piece of apple pie and ice cream. Then they served the main course. How much appetite would you have for the main course? Probably none, because the apple pie and the ice cream would have satiated your appetite.

What would happen to your physical body, your levels of energy, and your health if every morning you started off with a big piece of apple pie and ice cream? You'd have less motivation. You'd have less energy. You'd get an energy surge, but it would decline if you didn't have any protein in your diet. You wouldn't be feeding your brain, so your brain would get tired very quickly. That's one of the reasons why it's so important to have a really nutritious breakfast, because that nutrition is the charging of your brain. It's the glucose; it's the energy to the brain that enables you to function at a high level.

When people start off with dessert in the workplace, for the rest of the day they waste time. They want more dessert. They send out more messages. They check their email continually. They go and talk to other people. They read the paper. They bother others. They can't get into work, because they've had this dessert.

Fully 50% of work time today is completely wasted in non-work activities. That's the average. Many people beat the average.

Highly productive people are way below the average. But the average is 50% wasted time.

If you ask people, by the way, whether they waste time at work, they'll say, "Absolutely not. I go in there; I hit it all day." So you say, "Well, as it happens, we've had a hidden camera on you for the last ten hours of your working day from the time you arrived to the time you quit. We'd like to sit down and play it back and see what it looks like."

Then you watch. The person comes to work. Do they go to work? No, the first thing they do is they go and meet and greet and talk to their coworkers as if they haven't seen them for six months. Then they go like hummingbirds from flower to flower; they go from person to person, reestablishing their relationship. *How are you doing? How is everything going? What did you do last night? What did you see on television? Oh, that looks nice. Where did you get that?* Finally the person realizes they had better get some work done before the boss comes by.

You find the average person today does not start work until 11:00 a.m. Then, at about a quarter to twelve, they start to wind down for lunch. Then they have a sixty-minute lunch, and they take ninety minutes.

They come back at 1:30, and they have to reestablish all their friendships in the office. They haven't seen these people for ninety minutes, so they go like a hummingbird from person to person, having a little chat. Finally they realize, "Gee, I had better get some work done," so about 2:30 or 3:00, they do a little bit of work. Then they start to wind down at 3:30.

Sometimes I joke. You ever get caught in rush hour traffic? Rush hour traffic in Los Angeles starts at 3:30. The 401, one of the major freeways, turns into a parking lot. If you get onto the freeway after 3:30, you're going to be there for hours. What would otherwise take you sixty minutes will take you five to six hours.

Now who are all these people? These are all people who don't get off until 5:00. What they're doing is trying to beat the traffic home by getting onto the freeway by 3:30.

My point is that people waste their time. If you ask them, they say, "No, no." It's called *invisible time wastage*. It's only when you play back the recording and you have a meter counting the minutes and seconds at the bottom that they'll say, "Well, I said hello to so-and-so when he came in." Seventeen minutes and three seconds saying hello to so-and-so.

Go on to the next person, eleven minutes and four seconds. Go on to the next person, fifteen minutes and twenty-five seconds. When they see these camera playbacks, people are shocked. They had no idea that they were wasting most of their time.

Now how do you this? First thing you do in the morning is check your email. You check your email, you have your dessert, and from then on, your day is a dessert day. It's chatting with your friends and having fun and going out for lunch and reading the paper and seeing what's for sale on eBay and checking more email and sending messages to people and getting messages back. It's checking your Facebook and sending cartoons and jokes that you picked up on Facebook.

The average working person today spends one to two hours of every working day on Facebook, just chatting and talking to their friends. Then they answer their business emails, and then they send out emails to get replies back, and so on. At the end of the day, they look at the camera. They almost want to throw up.

What you're doing is you're destroying your future. You're destroying all your hopes and dreams for the future simply by wasting so much time, because you don't have this long-term perspective.

So start your day with a very clear schedule, planned and structured. Set priorities on that schedule, and then put your head down and hit it, and hit it hard all day long. When you walk in you wave—hi, everybody!—and go straight to work.

One of my great rules, which I stumbled across many years ago, is *work all the time you work*. Someone says, "Hey, have you got a minute to talk right now?" "I'd love to. Let's talk after work. Right now I have to get back to work."

Back to work. Back to work. Whenever you find yourself drifting, keep saying *back to work, back to work*.

People ask, "How do you do it?" "Look, I have to get this job done. I have to get back to work. I'll talk to you later."

Pretty soon they leave you alone. Pretty soon they find that you're not really interesting. You're not ready to sit and hang for indefinite periods of time. So, walk in, say hello, and go straight to work. Put your head down and work all the time you work.

When you've finished your work, then raise your head, and then you can talk to people and chat with people. Let them ruin their careers, but don't let them ruin yours.

Dan

Outstanding. Those are some great ideas for sustaining motivation. I also love your reward system to keep people motivated, because there can be a time when you hit that desert, and that's when you need those little motivators to keep you going.

You were talking about email, Brian, and as we know, today email is just one of many virtual forms of communication. People have their smartphones with them all day long, whether they're professionals or they're teenagers.

It seems that everywhere you go, people have their laptops open. They have their mobile phones with them. There's social media, there's texting, there's email, there's all of these types of electronic communication. This constant "white noise" of 24/7 communications and alerts is pushing people into a sense of urgency. It seems that more and more, our society, even our workplaces slowly have succumbed to this danger.

Building upon what you said about email, how do we develop this long-term perspective, when we have all of these devices in our lives that are constantly pulling us into that urgency? People sometimes expect an instantaneous response. How do you set your life up in a way that that stuff doesn't pull you away from your goals?

Brian

The most powerful tool you have is your ability to think and your ability to think *in advance*. I sometimes ask, what is the most valuable and highest paid work that you do? It's thinking. It's thinking about the consequences of your behaviors: if I do this, what is likely to happen?

In fact, the ability to accurately predict the consequences of your behavior before you act is the highest mark of intelligence. The person who can play down the chessboard of life and calculate, "If I do this, life will do that, then I will do this, I'll have to do that," and so on. All successful people play several steps ahead.

As for email, when you get an email, it's very much like a slot machine. With a slot machine, you pull it, and it goes ding, ding, ding. You don't know what's going to happen. Are you going to win? Are you going to lose? You're in anticipation of the surprise.

They've found that it's exactly the same mentality, that shiny-object mentality, when you have your email on, and it goes off and it goes *bing. You have an email.* It immediately stops you from whatever you're doing. You say, "Oh, I wonder what I won. Maybe it's a friend, maybe it's funny, maybe it's a joke." What happens is you stop.

I read a book on brain function recently, and it said that there are two major obstacles to proper brain functioning today. Number one is distraction. We are distracted by so many things, especially electronic distractions.

The second is multitasking. Multitasking is where you're trying to do several things at once. There are several books and articles written on the myth of multitasking. It *is* a myth, because we don't multitask. Instead we task-shift, so we're focused like a light beam on this task, and then we get a bing, and we switch to the computer to check the email. Then we switch back, but it takes between seven and seventeen minutes for you to get back to your task.

Now here's an interesting discovery, and one of my favorites: all success in life comes from task completion. It does not come from working on tasks. It comes from completing tasks.

Eighty-two percent of Americans would like to write a book sometime. They would like to be published authors; they would like to tell their stories, personally or about their profession. They dream of writing a book and having it g in print. Some of them even take a run at it. But they never complete it.

The world is full of incomplete manuscripts, incomplete poems, incomplete business plans. People don't complete them. But it's task completion that's the key to success.

Here's a tremendous way to promote a long-term perspective, and to become more successful. When you start off in the morning, imagine that your workday starts at 8:30. The first thing you do is make a list of everything you have to do that day before you begin. You never start work without a list. The best thing is to make the list the night before.

If something new comes up, write it on the list before you do it. Don't get thrown off track by a shiny object, somebody calling you, texting you, or anything else. Write it down before you do it.

Then, let's say you start work at 8:30. You're planned, prepared, you look at your task list, and you say, "If I could only do one job on this list before I was called out of town for a month, which one would I want to be sure to complete?" Then you start work on that, and you put your head down, and you work nonstop for ninety minutes. You turn off your television, your phone, your computer, everything. Put your head down and work nonstop for ninety minutes.

Then get up, give yourself a break, walk around, get a cup of coffee or tea, for fifteen minutes. Then come back and sit down and hit it again for another ninety minutes. Then check your email. Your email is your dessert. You've now had dinner.

If you can do two flat-out ninety-minute work sessions without interruption or distraction every morning, you will double and then triple and then quadruple your productivity, and eventually your income. You will complete more and more tasks. You'll become known as the go-to person.

Many years ago, I had this great experience. I was struggling and working my way up, and I put together a real estate deal, and I managed to tie up the property. But I didn't have any money.

So I began visiting development companies, and I finally stumbled across one. They said, "If your numbers hold up, we'd be interested in coming in with you as a partner."

I had read all the books; there were twenty-one books on real estate development. I knew exactly how to put together a pro forma. I hired a professional typist, because I didn't have a typewriter, and to follow it out, I put together this proposal.

I sat down with their real estate development lawyers. I showed them I had corroboration for every single number and statement in the account. I had letters of intent from major tenants. I had letters of cost analysis from a construction company. I had every single cost, every single source of revenue, all the percentage point returns, how much they would make if it was fully leased, and so on.

At the end they said, "This is the most complete business proposal we've ever seen." They checked it all out, and they said, "OK, we'll come in. We'll pay 100% of all the costs of developing this shopping center for 75% ownership, leaving you 25% to carry it through to completion." I did, and they did. It was the most incredible damned thing.

Not long after that, the president of this company, one of the richest and most respected men in Canada, called me into his office. He said, "I like the way you work. I like your work ethic, your qualifications. You fulfilled every promise that you ever made on schedule. How would you like to come and work for me as my personal assistant?"

I thought about it, and I thought this might be the greatest opportunity of my life. So we arranged a deal, and I went to work for him as his personal assistant. He would give me little assignments to do, almost like a mentee. He'd never had a personal assistant before, so I had to ask him, "I need something to do. I want something more to do," and he would give me something to do.

Whatever it was, I'd run out and do it immediately and bring it back, almost like a dog racing for a throwing stick and racing back. And he would nod and smile. He didn't say very much. He'd smile. Then a few days later, he'd give me something else to do.

These were little things, but whatever he gave me to do, I ran out and did it and came back immediately. He said, "Boy, that was fast. You really take this seriously. It's not that important. Next week would be fine."

But then a big opportunity came up, and he said, "Do you want to take a look at this?" It turned into a $25 million importation and distribution company, and he made me the president of it.

Another opportunity came up—a major real estate development, several hundred acres, homes, industrial parks, commercial, residential, everything. "Would you like to take a look at this?" I jumped all over that and put a plan together and brought it back to him. So he put me in charge of this new development.

Then he said, "We're planning on building a downtown office building, and we're not exactly sure how it should be configured, what the cost should be, what the rents will be. Would you like to take a look at that?" Pretty soon I was in charge of developing a twelve-story office building in the center of downtown.

He kept giving me assignments. Every time he gave me an assignment, I would jump all over it and do it immediately. And

I worked all the time I worked. I was working ten or twelve hours a day.

By the end of my time with him, when he retired, I was running three major divisions of the company. I was making more money than I'd ever dreamed of in my life. I had received more experience than I ever thought. I had a staff of forty-two working in my three divisions. I had the biggest office in the company next to his.

I was beyond everyone else who worked in this large conglomerate. They were jealous of me, and are jealous to this day. The only thing I had was when they gave me a task, I did it, and I did it fast, and I did it 100%. If you wanted something done in a month or two, give it to one of the other people. If you wanted it done now and you wanted it done quickly and well, give it to Brian. Whatever you give to Brian, no matter how busy he is, he'll get all over it and get it done.

That's the way you develop a long-term perspective. I realized that I wasn't working just for the short term; I was working to develop myself and my skills and my abilities for the long term. After I left this gentleman, we remained friends forever, and I was ten years further along in my career than I could ever have dreamed possible. I had more experience and knowledge. I was able to earn more money. I went on to develop $100 million worth of real estate with the skills that I had learned under his supervision and under his tutelage.

The long-term perspective means you work really hard in the short term, work every single day, putting in two ninety-minute sessions every morning. You start work and hit it; work all the time you work. Give yourself rewards and gratification. "Once I put in three solid hours, then I'll check my email, because email is dessert. Then I'll take myself out for lunch. I deserve lunch now because I've done this work."

When you come back, hit it again. Develop the reputation in your company for being the hardest-working person in your organization. Say they brought in an outside firm of management consultants, and they questioned everybody in the office, and asked, "Who is the hardest worker here?" You be sure that you win. You're going to win the vote. You're going to win at the convention, and nobody else knows that this contest is going on. Nobody else knows that the researchers are coming in. Your job is to win, because nothing will move you ahead faster in your career than to be known as the hardest-working, most productive person in your business.

Dan

That's outstanding advice. Wow. I'm ready to run out and get to work myself. Can we talk about this as it relates to teenagers? I know a lot of parents are reading this. They're reading for their professions, but they're also thinking about the kids that they're raising. I know your kids are older now, but a lot of teenagers these days are so addicted to their phones. They spend their whole lives there.

Mark Bauerlein, who wrote a fascinating book called *The Dumbest Generation*, basically said that never has a generation been more privileged to have more access to education, but they spend most of their time on junk—junk videos, pornography, all sorts of horrible things. So the question the parents have is, what is the best thing I can do for my preteen or teenager to get them to a point where they can, if you will, pass the marshmallow test?

They're being saturated in this digital world like a fish swimming in water.

Is there something specific you would advise parents to do for preteens or teenagers that are addicted to this digital life, and it's interfering with their grades or other important things?

Brian

Yes. The way to become the most important influence in your child's life is to become the most important source of emotional support and unconditional love. They will be influenced by their peers and by their friends in school and people they meet, but they always have to know that you are the most important person in their lives in terms of how totally dedicated you are to them.

What is it that everybody wants to feel? Everybody wants to feel like a winner. If you feel like a winner, you have high self-esteem. The more you win, the more confidence you have, the happier you are, the more respected you are.

How do you get the winning feeling? The answer is, you win. That's how you get the winning feeling.

How do you win? You cross the finish line.

In work, you set up the job, and you break it down into smaller pieces. Let me give you an example.

Many companies used to reward their salespeople when they made the sale, but sometimes if the sale was, say, a large piece of equipment, it would take five to seven months. That was the sales cycle, from the time you contacted the prospect and went through the bidding process and the submission process and the design process and the installation process. Then the salesperson would get the reward.

This was obviously causing a lot of demotivation, because the salespeople weren't getting any payoff for all the work they were doing. So the companies divided this sales process into seven parts. The first part was actually coming face-to-face and identifying a real life prospect who wanted and needed and could pay for the product. That was a source of celebration, and they would give hands of applause for having opened the door, cracked the ice, and started the process.

The next step would be the submission of an initial bid based on an analysis of the client's situation. They would get rewards based on that. In short, every time they completed a step, they were made to feel like a winner.

We found the same thing with our children. Every single thing that our children have ever done, started, and completed, whether it's cleaning up their room or painting a picture in kindergarten or reading a book, we make a big thing of it. Wow! Holy smokes!

When my first daughter, Christina, brought home her first painting from school, which was a stick painting of people, I said, "Did Christina do this? Christina, did you do this? Who helped you on this? This is far too good a painting for you to have done on your own."

She was five years old. She said, "No, I did it all by myself, Dad." "I can't believe it. That is incredible. Look how good it is! Can we put this up on the refrigerator? I want to be able to see this every time I come into the kitchen. Would you help me put it up on the refrigerator, Christina?" We put it up on the refrigerator, and every time we went by, we'd say, "Look at that!"

Somebody came in to visit. I said, "Let me show you something. This is a painting that my daughter, Christina, did. Isn't it beautiful? Isn't she smart?" Christina just basked in this.

I raised three more children, Glen, David, and Catherine. I've done the same thing every time they do something little. I make a fuss over it so they feel like winners.

If you do that, eventually they will strive for opportunities to win. They become impatient with playing online, with being a "screenager." They become impatient. They really want to get good grades. They want to do things that make them feel like winners, because their parents have always made them feel like winners when they completed a task.

In the Bible it says, "O good and faithful servant, you have been faithful over small things. I will make you master over many." If you praise and encourage your children when they do little things, they will do bigger and bigger things, and they'll be much more easily distracted from their friends who are doing useless stuff. They'll say, "It's time to go. I have to go home now. I have to get back to work. I have to get my assignment done. I have to get this complete."

You don't even have to influence them or threaten them or demand. Because they feel so good about themselves, they'll just go out and get good grades all by themselves.

Dan

Excellent advice. You've talked a bit about time management. One framework for time management that really has helped a lot of people focus on the long term was introduced by Stephen Covey in his book *The Seven Habits of Highly Effective People* and picked up from A. Roger and Rebecca Merrill. It has to do with the four quadrants.

I was wondering if you could explain the concept of the four quadrants, especially quadrant 2. And how if a person organizes their life around quadrant 2, it can encourage them to design their life around the long term toward achieving their goals.

Brian

The quadrant theory of time management breaks everything you do into four parts. Imagine a box divided in half and half again, so there are four squares. You number the squares: 1, the upper left-hand square; 2, the upper right-hand square; 3, the lower left-hand square; and 4, the lower right-hand square. Now you have four quadrants.

Then you divide them up based on urgency and importance. The degree of importance runs down the left side, so you can say quadrant number 1 is important. U, urgent, is at the top, so this quadrant is both important and urgent. This is quadrant 1. It's on the upper left. It's called the Quadrant of Immediacy. This is almost always determined by external forces—commitments, things that you have to do and you have to get done *now*: meetings you have to go to, customers you have to call, and so on.

Most people spend their lives in quadrant 1. They are doing things that are immediate and important. By the way, if you don't do these things, they can be very dangerous for your job. If you don't get that assignment done, if you don't bring in those sales, if you don't complete a particular task, you could lose your job, so this is where you start. You always work in the Quadrant of Immediacy.

Now the next quadrant over, the one in the upper right, is quadrant number 2. It's the quadrant of things that are important but not urgent. This is called the Quadrant of Effectiveness. These are the things that have long-term potential consequences in your life: upgrading your skills, taking additional courses, writing out proposals and plans and reports, reading books and articles, and so on.

Anything that you do that is not urgent but important is in quadrant 2. Now everything that's in quadrant 2 can be delayed. You *can* procrastinate about it, but whatever's in quadrant 2 that is not urgent will soon become urgent.

A perfect example is in college. They will tell you at the beginning of the course that 50% of your final grade will be determined by your final paper. You must submit this paper by 8:00 in the morning on this date, or you will lose 50% of your credit for this course.

They repeat this every week. Remember, 50% of your grade will depend on your final paper. Do not delay. Do not procrastinate. Begin working on it now. Get it done early.

So what happens? Well, 90% of students put it off and put it off and put it off because it's not urgent yet. It's important. It's very important; it determines their whole success in this course, which may even amount to their whole success in the year. But they put it off and put it off.

When are most final papers written? The night before. I did this when I was taking an MBA degree. I'd come home at 5:00 p.m. I'd make a big pot of coffee, and I'd sit down at my little kitchen table, and I'd begin writing. I'd write all night, and I'd just keep pouring the coffee. Then, as the sun would come up, I'd get in my car. I'd race over to the university and to the professor's office and slip the final paper under his door.

When I'd look under his door, it was jammed with final papers. Everybody did it at the last minute. The point is that for a long time the paper was important, but it wasn't urgent. But at a certain point it became extremely urgent—more urgent than anything else.

What Covey said, and what the Merrills said, is to get everything done in quadrant 1, the things you have to do now. Then start doing things in quadrant 2 that have long-term potential consequences.

Quadrant 3, on the lower left, includes those activities that are urgent but not important. These are people talking to you, emails, somebody coming to your desk, chatting with people, going for lunch, and so on. These are urgent because they're right in your face, but they're not important. This is called the Quadrant of Delusion.

This means you're at work, and you're interacting with people, so you delude yourself into thinking *I'm actually working. This is part of my employment. This is what I need to do to get along with my coworkers. I need to have fun at work.*

Anybody who tells you that you need to have fun at work is a loser, a person who has no future. This person is going to retire poor, is going to have to live on pensions, and will probably go to a senior citizens' home, where nobody will visit them. Anybody who tells you that work is supposed to be a fun place is a person who's not serious about their future.

It's not that you don't enjoy your coworkers. It's not that you don't laugh with your coworkers, but you do it within the context of working together to get the job done, not just sitting around shooting the breeze. In the Quadrant of Delusion, people delude themselves into thinking they are working when what they're doing is totally, 100%, useless time.

The fourth quadrant, on the lower right, is the quadrant where it's neither urgent nor important, and this is called the Quadrant of

Waste. Reading the newspaper, checking through random emails, looking for what's for sale, calling home to see what's for dinner, and things like that.

Most people spend most of their time in quadrants 3 and 4. Your job is to switch it over. Spend all of your time in quadrants 1 and 2. Get everything done as quickly as you possibly can that must be done now, that's both important and urgent, and then spend more and more time in quadrant 2. Those activities have long-time value, and can make a huge difference in your business.

Dan

Brian, we've gotten a lot of great ideas here on long-term perspective and delaying gratification. We want to finish with a closing thought, one thought to leave people with about how to develop that long-term perspective.

Brian

Going through the goal setting exercise that we talked about earlier, you pick your most important goal in life. You can have a personal goal in your personal life: your family. You can have a health goal, and you can have a business or career goal. Say, "What is my biggest and most important business or career goal?"—the one which is going to connect directly to your income, your speed of promotion, your level of respect in the company.

Then you say, "What's the most important activity that I can engage in right now to achieve my most important work goal?" That becomes where you start at the beginning of the day. You discipline yourself to start there, before you check your email or anything else. You discipline yourself to work nonstop on that one task until it's complete, and you do this over and over again (we'll talk about rituals a little bit later). You do this over and over again until it becomes automatic for you to sit down and start work on your most important task, and then just work on it full blast until it's complete.

Once you develop that habit of completing your most important task first thing in the morning, you'll become one of the most productive, most respected, and highest paid people in your field.

EIGHT

Sustaining Motivation, Part Three: The Keys to Resilience When Life Gets Tough

Dan

Brian, here we're going to cover the really difficult moments, not just the minor irritations that life can throw your way on a daily basis, but the real, significant difficulties that people go through in life. Let's discuss how you can sustain your motivation through something that might take you off track, if you are not prepared. I'd like to begin by discussing how Murphy's Law applies to both our business and personal lives and how we must expect that, despite our best motivation and planning, life is going to throw us at least one or two major curveballs, if not more, during our lifetimes.

You might even want to start out by discussing some of the business challenges you had when you were young, facing bankruptcy, and health challenges you've had recently, and what you did to sustain your motivation during times like this.

Brian

Earlier we talked about the role of expectations in motivation, attitude, performance, and behavior. Expectations determine your level of resilience, your level of persistence, everything. So we always have to ask, what are your expectations?

Here's an example. Harvard found that leaders hate the idea of losing. They hate the idea of failing, but they know that it is impossible to achieve anything worthwhile without making mistakes, without losing, without having setbacks and difficulties. So they plunge forward nonetheless.

I began studying this form of psychology many years ago, as I told you, and I spent thousands of hours in it. One thing I discovered, which was so profound for me, was what is called *preprogramming*. You can actually preprogram your subconscious mind well in advance of the incident so that when the incident does occur, you're ready. As we said, it's like taking a first aid course well in advance of the accident, so when the accident occurs, you're ready.

One thing you can preprogram yourself for is for the fact that you will have countless mistakes, failures, challenges, obstacles, difficulties, setbacks, disappointments. These are inevitable and unavoidable parts of an active life. The only way you *cannot* have these things is if you go and sit in a room by yourself. Even then, you could have all kinds of problems.

So you say, "I'm going to have all kinds of problems and difficulties in my life, but I am never going to let them get me down. No matter what happens, I will bounce back from it. I will find a way through it or around it. I will try again or try something different."

Just say that to yourself. It helps to say that to yourself repeatedly. Then the next time you have an obstacle, when you have a letdown or a disappointment, you feel as if you've had a punch in the emotional solar plexus. You feel stunned, disappointed, knocked back on your heels. The only question is, how long do you stay there?

Everybody has this shock of disappointment when something that they expected to go well goes poorly. The question is, how quickly do you bounce back? If you have preprogrammed yourself, you automatically bounce back. But if you had this idea that things should be fine, and things should work out, life should be good, and then it isn't, your disappointment, the clash between your expectation and the reality, causes you to become depressed and angry and lash out.

I've actually written a whole book on this, which we'll talk about a little later when we come to crisis management. In fact, I'm now speaking all over the world to companies on my business courses, and they're asking me to put in a one-hour or two-hour module on crisis management, crisis anticipation, crisis thinking. What can you do to think clearly and effectively and get better results in any crisis in your business life?

The critical thing is the gap between expectations and reality. If you expect that life is going to be difficult, and you're going to have lots of unexpected setbacks and difficulties but you're not going to let them get you down, then, when they happen, you don't. You just automatically bounce back.

Dan

Wonderful, wonderful. So there are two different mind-sets when it comes to dealing with setbacks. One is from the famous

M. Scott Peck book *The Road Less Traveled*, and it begins with the provocative statement "Life is difficult." Once you've understood and accepted that, then in a sense life no longer becomes difficult, because you're ready for anything that comes your way.

The other side is a more New Age approach, or maybe it comes from something like *The Power of Positive Thinking*. It's reframing the situation by saying life really isn't that difficult. When you think about it, it's actually not that hard. It's all a matter of my mind-set. If I perceive it as difficult, that's a problem. You change it to more of a life is easy, life is flowing, approach.

So there are two different approaches. One is facing the difficulty and accepting it, and the other is using your mind for mental gymnastics, if you will. I'm curious which approach you favor and why you think one is superior to another.

Brian

Well, they're both positive. But let's go back to your suggestion earlier about Murphy's Law. Murphy's Law is the funny law that says whatever can go wrong, will go wrong.

The first corollary of Murphy's Law is whatever can go wrong, will go wrong, and will cost the most amount of money. The second corollary is whatever can go wrong, will go wrong, and will take the most amount of time. Then there's Smith's Law, which said that Murphy was an optimist.

I work with thousands of business owners, and I give them the two and three rule: everything that you plan in your business is going to end up costing you twice as much and will take three times as long—especially if you're starting a business and you're looking toward getting to break even, the point where you'll be able to make more profits than it's costing you. Even if you have a good business mind, it's going to take you twice as long as your best calculations, and it's going to cost you three times as much money, or vice versa. It's always three and two, two and three.

I have people come back to me who started a business. They said, "You know, I listened to that and I said, 'No. That may be true for him or for other people, but not for me.' I knew it wasn't going to apply to me, but it did." Everything takes twice as long, costs three times as much, or costs three times as much and takes twice as long.

So you build that into your calculations. By doing that, when you find that your best expectations don't work out, you're not disappointed or destroyed, because in the back of your mind, you said, "I sort of knew this was going to happen." You can actually program yourself so that when things do go wrong, you can dance around them like a boxer and not let them knock you down.

Look for the good in every situation. If you have a setback or difficulty, say, "That's good." Then you look into it, and you say. "What could be good about this?"

Very often your greatest success is going to come from what appears to be a great failure. Sometimes people will start a business and go bankrupt, but the lessons they learned from that business enable them to be financially successful, maybe even millionaires, later. Then you look back, and you say, "Thank heavens that first business went broke. It was in the wrong industry. Everybody got into that industry and lost everything. We lost, but we lost a small amount in a short period of time. So that was good luck for us. Thank heavens. It's almost like somebody was looking over us to help us to fail." There's a rule that says, *fail fast, learn quickly, try again*.

I was giving a seminar in Stockholm last year. Four VIPs had paid a special extra fee to have lunch with me during the seminar. So I sat down with them. These people were software engineers.

They were obviously a little bit concerned. They said, "We need your advice. You've worked with so many companies." I said, "All right, what is it?"

"We've been selling this software program, and we found that this business model wasn't working. Sales were difficult. So we created a new business model. The new business model is that we are going to lease the program and service it, so there'll be a much lower upfront initial cost for the client. Not only that, if there are any problems, we'll take care of them, so it's going to be a much easier, cheaper, and ultimately, a more profitable product, because we'll be able to sell far more of them."

"So what is your problem?" I said.

"It's not going well. Our revenues are down, our sales force is disagreeing. The customers that we've spoken to are used to owning it. Now they're being told they can't own it; they can only lease it."

I said, "According to Peter Drucker, every new business model requires four iterations before you get it right. Sometimes it's much more, but it's a minimum of four. You've only tried one. You have three more different ways of doing it before you get to the average."

You should just have seen the smiles of relief that went over their faces. They said, "Thank you so much for telling us that, because we had this expectation that if this was a good, new business model, it should work immediately. "

"No, don't worry." I said. "It's like preparing a recipe in the kitchen. No matter how good a cook you are, the first time you prepare a recipe, it's not going to taste that great. So what you have to do is go back, and you have to change some of the components and some of the ingredients and some of the proportions, and you have to try it again and get feedback and taste it and see what happens. You have to do this a minimum of four times before it starts to taste good. Same thing with a new business model." As I said earlier, sometimes it's fourteen times or forty times or 100 times, but you just keep working at it until it works perfectly.

This is an attitude that you have to have. Don't expect everything to work perfectly the first time. Don't expect your great idea to be a great idea.

One thing we teach in business is that ideas are a dime a dozen; people have hundreds of ideas. The very first thing that you apply is what is called *proof of concept*. You say, "I have a great idea for a product or a service or a price or a way that we can market or sell and grow the business."

You say, "Great. That's an idea. The idea has no value at all. Everybody has ideas; there are millions of them. Now you have to prove that it's true."

How do you prove that it's true? You go to the person you expect to consume your product or service, and you give it to them. You ask them, "Do you like it? Would you buy it? Does it make you happy? Is this better than our competitors' products? If so, why? If not, why not? What changes do we have to make?"

This is the cutting edge of the future today: you begin with the confidence that your first iteration's not going to work, or your second, or your third, or your fourth.

When I started off in sales, when I was twenty-three and knocking on doors, I was selling a small item. It cost $20. It was a membership in a bonus club, where you got this little card, like a credit card, and you took it to one of more than 100 restaurants, and you would get a 10% or 20% discount on your dinner.

So it could pay for itself in one use. One businessman could go out with a couple of other businesspeople or their families, and in one or two uses it more than paid for itself. It was an easy sell. Pay $20, and you could use it indefinitely for a year. You could save hundreds and hundreds of dollars. The payoff was tremendous.

Well, I thought, like most young salespeople, everybody would buy this. All I have to do is hold it up and tell them what it was, and they'd rip it out of my hand.

So I went out and began knocking on doors, and everybody said no. "No, I don't want it. No, I can't afford it. Not in the market right now. I'd probably never go to any of those restaurants." They had every single excuse in the book, and everybody said no or some version of no.

I went from door to door to door, hour after hour, from door to door. Finally someone said to me, "You know this is quite normal. When you start off, you'll get an enormous amount of rejection. What you have to do is you have to get more rejection. You have to understand that sales is a failure game, not a success game. It's a game of nos. It's a game of probabilities. Your job is to fail more often."

So I used to run between calls. I'd run between offices, and when I was prospecting in the neighborhoods, I'd run between homes. I would actually run almost like a runner, a messenger, so I could get rejected more often. I kept doing this and doing this until I finally hit on a method of selling, and within one day, my sales had tripled.

But I was pushing and pushing, realizing that this is not a sales game. It's a failure game. You're going to fail over and over and over again to be successful. Once you have that attitude, nothing can stop you.

When I teach salespeople, I say, "If you want to get your sales career or your company's sales force really revved up, have a contest. We call it the 100-call contest. Everybody makes a commitment to go out and make 100 calls as fast as they can without worrying about whether or not they make any sales. A call is actually speaking to a prospect, whether it's on the telephone or face-to-face. Whoever gets to 100 calls first, the company pays for them and their spouse to go out to the best restaurant in town."

You make it a game, and every day, everybody comes back and reports on the number of calls that they've made. Everybody's racing to be the one that wins the dinner out at the first class restaurant. Nobody cares if they sell; they just care about getting those numbers. And the sales explode.

Dan

Wow.

Brian

I remember I was working with this company. They were all telephone marketing. So they put this system in place. The first person who could get ten nos in the morning once they started would have their lunch paid for by the company.

They'd all line up like horses at the gate, everybody ready with their telephones. Ready, and at 8:30, someone would say, "Go." Everybody would start dialing, dialing, dialing, until finally somebody would jump up and ring the bell. They'd made ten calls and gotten ten rejections faster than anyone else.

They'd turn to the other ones and say, "What happened to you?" "I called somebody, and they wanted to buy, and I had to take the time to take the order and get the money." "Me too, I made two sales. I just couldn't get to the ten nos because everybody kept wanting to buy."

Every time a company uses this, they're astonished. First of all, everybody's laughing, so the person on the other end of the phone hears the laugh. The person's positive, smiling, happy. They don't care if you buy; they just want to get through this call.

They say, "Tell me more about that product. That sounds really good. I was thinking of something like this. How much does it cost? How do I get it?" They begin to sell and sell.

The owner of this company retired as a multimillionaire six years later at the age of fifty. He moved to Palm Springs, and he plays golf every day. He said he never made so much money in his whole life as when nobody cared about rejection.

Dan

That is great. That's almost like what they call exposure therapy, when you expose yourself to the thing you think you most fear.

You talk about a resilient mind-set, this ability to face your fear. Are there other specific qualities that you've seen in resilient people that stand out?

Brian

I put together a program on crisis management some years ago during the crisis of 2001. I upgraded the program in 2006, 2007, and now I speak all over the world in countries that are going through dramatic crises. They ask me, "Please talk about crisis," so I pulled out the very best ideas I had.

I'm the only person who'd ever written a book on the subject, by the way, and it's called *Crunch Point: The Twenty-One Secrets to Succeeding When It Matters Most*. Number one is when something goes wrong, stay calm. Just stay calm.

Over the years, I've worked as a consultant and advisor, and I'd even say I've been a friend to some very wealthy people, including multi-multimillionaires and billionaires. I've worked with them at times where there are big challenges or crises within their companies. Something's going seriously wrong, something completely unexpected. I watch them, and I watch how they handle it. I would get emotional and upset myself, because I really care for my clients.

I would watch them, and they would all go calm. Every top person I ever met would go dead calm in the middle of a crisis.

Why? You do all of your thinking with your neocortex, the frontal cortex of the brain, and this is what makes us uniquely human. This is where we think and we analyze and we compare, and then we decide.

As long as you are calm, your full frontal cortex is on full blast. It's lit up; it's working. But as soon as you become angry or emotional, it shuts down. Just like turning off all the lights in a building.

You revert to your limbic system, which is fight or flight. It's stimulated by your emotions: anger, fear, lashing out, blaming. All these negative emotions suddenly become dominant in your thinking. But as soon as you calm down and take a deep breath, your limbic system, the emotions, settle down. The lobes of your prefrontal cortex all open up, and you start to see things with greater clarity.

I've heard about great generals in warfare, with incredible attacks and counterattacks and people dying: they become as calm as death. They think clearly, and they direct the battle calmly and clearly. Whereas sometimes their enemies get angry and upset. They make the wrong decisions, and it can be cataclysmic.

So the starting point in dealing with a crisis at any time is to stay calm. The next thing is to get the facts. Whenever you're in a crisis, stop, take a time-out, and get the facts. Never believe what you've heard. Find out if it is a real problem. Find out if the problem is as grim as they said. Find out, because nothing is ever as bad as it seems initially. Nothing is ever as good as it seems initially. So get the facts and ask questions.

Here's the most remarkable thing: it's impossible for you to ask intelligent questions and be angry or upset at the same time. The very act of asking questions calms you down, activates your frontal lobe, and makes you see things clearly. Also, it calms everybody else down.

The mark of the leaders is that, whenever they have a big setback or difficulty, they say, "All right, let's sit down here. What exactly has happened here, and how do we know that's true? Has anybody checked or corroborated that that is actually what happened? When did this occur? How did this happen at this time? What are the exact steps that occurred, and who was involved in this? Who could we talk to about resolving this? What are the steps that we could take now? What steps could we take to minimize the potential damage or loss?"

As you keep asking these questions, everybody settles down, and their frontal lobes activate as well. Pretty soon, you have a whole group of people thinking calmly and clearly and rationally about the actions that you can take immediately to minimize the cost of the crisis.

Another thing in crisis management is always to accept responsibility, as we've said before. The natural tendency is to blame other people or circumstances when things go wrong, but as we said earlier, if you do, you immediately become angry. All negative emotions are based on blame, and the antidote to blame is accepting responsibility.

So people on my staff will come into my office, and they'll say, "I have this problem; this happened. These people cheated us." I'll say, "Hold on. Calm down. You are responsible. This is your area of responsibility, so let's analyze this. What exactly happened? How did it happen? What are you going to do? What is your next step?" Instead of having them come and hand the problem off to me, I turn it around, and I push it back into their hands.

Over time, the most amazing thing happens. They say, "There's this problem" (there are always problems in business), and they say it in a calm way. "This is what happened, and I am responsible, so this is what I've decided to do."

Then they explain their plan of action. They say, "What do you think of that?" And I say, "That's very good." In most cases, they're closest to the problems, so their idea is better than anyone else's.

But sometimes I'll say, "You know, I've seen this problem before, and you might think of doing this as well." They go, "Ah, that's a great idea. I hadn't thought of that." They do that one additional thing, and they walk away proud, confident; their minds are clear and calm. There's no blame or anger from me.

Stuff happens in business. People cheat you, things don't go through, sales don't work, and so on. Just stay calm and manage it. You can do this with any major problem in life. You make the decision in advance that no matter what happens, you're going to remain calm and clear and ask questions and find a solution and take action on it.

Dan

That's almost a meditative way of approaching it, which is so great. You don't see it very often modeled in our culture, certainly not in our popular culture. We really need to look toward mentors, to those Level 5 leaders you were talking about before, for approaching situations like that.

Let's apply some of the ideas you just discussed to major life difficulties. There are two major fears that people have in life: the fear of public speaking and the fear of death.

All of these major losses that I'm going to ask you to discuss are deaths in one shape or form.

One is divorce—death of a marriage. Two is bankruptcy—the death of a business, at least in some cases. There are different types of bankruptcy, but in this case, I'm thinking about where somebody's facing going out of business.

Loss of a job. Loss of a parent. Loss of a spouse or child. Then, potentially losing your own life—a life-threatening diagnosis.

Let's look at each of those. I know you've faced some of these yourself or have known others who have been in very difficult situations like this. How specifically did they deal with these situations in order to bounce back? What are some strategies that might be specific to some of these circumstances?

Brian

Let's talk about divorce, or the breakup of a relationship. This can be an extremely emotional, traumatic event. In some cases, the couple can agree in a friendly way to go their own ways. But in many cases, it can be very nasty. The lawyers get involved, and they want you to fight as long as possible so they can earn as many fees as possible.

One thing that people don't realize is that lawyers earn their money from hourly fees. When you go to them with a problem, their goal is to make the meter run up as much as possible before you solve the problem. They'll want to do all kinds of depositions and all kinds of research and all kinds of follow-up.

So you go to a divorce lawyer. The divorce lawyer's job is to get you so spitting angry at the other person that you will run up the meter for a long time. They will get you to the point where you exaggerate everything bad that happened and how unjustified it was and how you are entitled to massive damages and compensation and so on. Just be aware of that.

Here's the most important point. When two people enter into a relationship, they enter into it with the best of intentions. Many relationships don't work out because people change and evolve in the course of the relationship.

Most divorces take place in the late twenties. People get married in their early twenties, and in that decade they go through the most rapid and dramatic period of change in their characters in their lives. At the end of the decade, they're not the same people that entered into the marriage at the beginning of the decade.

So you find that you are no longer compatible with the other person—and the true test of compatibility is how much you laugh together. The first thing that goes in a relationship is laughter. The sex, actually, is the thing that goes last. You can be going to divorce court, and you're still sleeping together, or sleeping together occasionally. The thing that goes last is the sex, but the first that goes is the humor.

You stop enjoying each other's company. There are long periods of silence when you're together. You watch television.

You sometimes see couples go out for dinner. They sit there, and they don't talk to each other. They look off. They check their phones. They sit there and eat, and then they get up and leave.

Incompatibility is something that just happens. It rains, the sun comes up, the grasses grow, and incompatibility occurs between people. Here's the point. No one is to blame. No one is at fault.

Both people enter into the relationship with the best of intentions. But because human beings change, they become different people; they find that they are no longer compatible. If that's the case, you take a deep breath, and you say, "Look, this isn't working out. I don't dislike you; you don't dislike me. You are not to blame. You're not at fault. Nobody's wrong here." It's the finding fault or blaming the other person that leads to all the turmoil in a divorce settlement.

But as soon as you realize that you both gave it the best shot, but you're not cut out for each other, it means that you're probably better cut out for someone else. The sooner you end this marriage and get on with the rest of your lives, the sooner you'll find a place where you'll be happy. That's the approach.

I was just having this conversation with a dear friend of mine in New York two weeks ago. Once you go through a divorce, there's going to be about a six-month period of healing. On average, it takes six months to heal after an emotional relationship has been terminated. So expect that.

Sometimes they talk about rebound relationships. People have rebound relationships right after the marriage or the relationship has ended. This rebound relationship is usually turbulent, unstable, and so on, but it's almost how they readjust to reality. At the end of six months, they're back to being their normal selves, and life goes on.

So what I would say about divorce is remember that nobody is at fault. Nobody's to blame. You just became incompatible, the same as it rains. It's a natural thing. No one is to be punished for it. Go your separate ways. Minimize it.

Go to a lawyer who specializes in working with couples and helping the couples to come to a happy situation where they resolve how to split up their property and their possessions, and so on. They do it in a gentlemanly, or if you like, in an adult way.

The second thing is bankruptcy. Now bankruptcy is very common. Most of the most successful people have been bankrupt. In fact, almost all wealthy people have been bankrupt, or almost bankrupt, two or three times. Henry Ford was bankrupt twice before he developed the Ford motor car. By the time he was sixty, he had become the richest man in the world.

A bankruptcy is painful. So what you have to do is, first of all, go through it. Go through it the best way you can, and remember life is very long. Never do or say anything in a divorce settlement or a bankruptcy that you don't want to live with for years. Don't say negative things to other people.

I've told friends of mine, "You're going through a divorce; never say a negative thing about the other person. Never say it to your children. Never say it to your friends. Always say these words:

he or she is an excellent person, but we found we were not suited for each other." That's the only thing you ever say, even if in your heart you're angry and disappointed.

For the bankruptcy, you recognize your reputation is the most important thing you have in your life. Your reputation with how you deal with money is very important. So if you go through a bankruptcy, treat everybody the best way you possibly can.

Do not sue. Do not accuse. Do not be angry. Just take it like an adult. It's sort of like taking a spanking. It's unfortunate. You did everything you possibly could.

Maybe you started a business when you didn't have enough experience. Maybe the market fell out from underneath you. But whatever happened, it's over. It's done. All that matters now is how you carry yourself. The most important thing in a bankruptcy is to ask, "What did I learn from this?"

I have a good friend who went through a business bankruptcy when he was in his mid-twenties. He spent two or three years building this business. He worked sixteen hours a day. He had two partners. And the business failed.

He had to move back in with his mother. It took him six months of mourning, basically six months of sitting around, watching television, before he got back on his feet.

But during that time, he did one of the smartest things I've ever heard of. He got a spiral notebook, and he wrote down the answers to these questions: *What did I learn from this business experience? What did I learn about people? What did I learn about customers? What did I learn about partners? What did I learn about marketing? What did I learn about money? What did I learn about banks? What did I learn about suppliers? What did I learn about credit?* And he would write down every lesson he'd learned in each of those categories.

He wrote them all down. He came up with ten or twenty lessons. I did this later myself, when I was going through a bad business situation. I just sat down and kept writing down all the lessons. Once you write down those lessons, you're ten times less likely to ever have those problems again, because writing the lessons down programs them into your subconscious mind.

Then when you see another situation that's similar to it, your subconscious mind goes, "Ding, ding, ding. We've been here before." You see it, and you ask questions, and you can save yourself a fortune.

So, after about six months writing down all these lessons and realizing what he had done right and what he would do differently, he started another business. Within a few years, he was a multimillionaire.

He said, "Identifying all my mistakes from my bankruptcy made me wealthy. The business would never have succeeded anyway in the long term, he said, but because it failed, it made me rich."

Then there's the loss of a job. Well, one of the rules is this: losing a job is God's way of telling you you're in the wrong position in the first place. Being fired is God's way of telling you you shouldn't even have had that job. So when you lose a job, you should consider it to be a blessing.

Peter Drucker has an interesting point here. He said keeping a person at a job in which they're incompetent is the cruelest thing you can do. He said if a person has no future at a job, and you've already decided that, let them go quickly. Let them go free so they can find a job that they're better suited for.

Many managers think that they're being compassionate by keeping a person in a job where they're obviously incompetent. I say no, you're just being cowardly. You're not being compassionate; you're being cruel and hurtful to this person. You're keeping them away from real life because when they finally do go, which they inevitably will, then they're going to have to start over.

The kindest, most loving, most gentle thing you can do with an employee who's not working out is set them free so they can find the right place for themselves. I've probably spoken to a million managers worldwide over the years. Eyes open up like sunrises when I tell them this. They realize, "Yes, the reason I've been keeping that person there is that I didn't want to hurt them or their family."

But you're killing these people. You're robbing them of the most important thing in the world, their lives, by keeping them off the field, sitting on the bench in a game that they're never going to be able to win.

Let them go free. Let them go freely. Help them. Give them support. Give them severance pay. Give them back everything, but let them go free.

I say to managers, the most astonishing thing that will happen is that this person will go to another company and get another job and will turn out to be a superstar. You'll say, "I fired that jerk two years ago, and look, he's now vice president of a fast-growing, high-tech company." Well, of course, but he wasn't right for your job.

The fourth area is the loss of a spouse or a child. This, again, is a traumatic area. It's sort of like a divorce. It takes six months for you to recover from that.

The most important thing is, don't blame yourself for anything. Don't say, "If only I'd done this or if only I'd done that," or "I should've spent more time with him or her," and so on. Don't beat yourself up when someone in your family dies, because when they die, it's over. It's finished.

Expect to take about six months to recover from that. Many people take six years. Many people never recover. They just walk around with a pall of gloom over their heads.

That's not for you. You accept that it's happened. You pray, if you want. Go for a walk. Take some time off. Relax. Read some spiritual material. And give yourself time to heal.

It's like breaking a limb: it takes time to heal. But the most beautiful words in the English language, the four words that are always true for all people at all times under all circumstances, are the words "This too shall pass."

Just say that. *This too shall pass.* It's very painful. It's hurtful. It's disappointing. You have all those what-ifs and what-ifs. But *this too shall pass.*

The last is a life-threatening diagnosis like cancer or heart disease. As you know, in 2010, I went to visit my doctor because I had this sniffle and runny nose. It had been going on for several weeks, so I thought I needed a Z-Pak or a bunch of penicillin to zap it out. I went in, and he did an analysis of it.

"Brian," he said, "I'll give you a Z-Pak, but I do not think you have a runny nose or an infection. I think you have throat cancer." I was shocked. Shocked.

Now of course, I'm a professional speaker, a narrator. Throat cancer. It was a shock to me, and I found that everybody who receives a cancer diagnosis goes into a period of shock, because the only thing they can think of is death. Death. Withering away and dying in great pain because of all the stuff that we've read and heard.

So I walked out stunned. I remember I was interviewing two potential clients that week on the phone for speaking engagements. I was so wired and upset, I was almost shouting into the phone when I was talking to them. Both of them said, "We don't want this guy anywhere near our people." It was the first time this had ever happened to me. Afterwards I could see that I was just so discombobulated with this diagnosis. So I really had to settle down.

Then I followed my own advice. Number one: stay calm. Number two: get the facts. I began to do enormous amounts of research. Over time I read more than thirty books on cancer. I went onto the websites; I checked every single part of WebMD, all the doctor sites, and everything on my type of cancer. I got all the information possible. I found that I had level 1, type 1 cancer. I had a melanoma in my throat.

Level 4 means it's over; select the roses for your funeral. Level 3 is the last chance, so you have to make it. I had level 1–level 2.

My doctors sat down and explained the standard of treatment. They said, "First, we'll do a biopsy to check to make sure that there is a genuine cancer and what it is. Second, we do chemotherapy, which will shrink the entire cancer area. Third, we will do surgery to take out any remaining cancerous parts that we can find. Fourth, you'll have radiation, which is a way of killing any invisible cancer cells that don't show up in MRIs.

"It's a six-month process. Parts of it are quite uncomfortable and painful. You'll lose your hair. Your throat will burn out. You'll lose your ability to swallow. You will lose your ability to taste anything, but if you follow this, at the end of six months, you'll be back speaking again."

So I followed their course of treatment. I kept reading everything I possibly could. I read about all the bogus treatments that are all over the Internet, none of which have ever been proven or validated by research, and I just followed the standard of treatment. Six months later, I was speaking to 800 people in Singapore and got a standing ovation.

So if you have a life-threatening disease, trust your doctors. Your doctors are not in this business to make a lot of money the way some of the cucks will say: "Oh, they found a cure; they're just keeping it hidden so they can make more money." I found that's totally untrue. The people within the cancer industry especially have committed their lives to saving people and to extending their lifespans.

Heart disease—it's the same thing. In every major category, the people dedicated their lives to helping their patients heal and live longer.

So trust your doctors. Do what they tell you. Relax. Stay calm. Stay informed. Get information.

The good doctors will say, "Go to another specialist, get a second opinion. Don't accept what I say." I did that. I got second opinions from one of the finest cancer centers in the United States. They came back and said, "What your doctor has recommended is exactly correct." So you just relax and say, "Take me." Six months later I was speaking.

So the critical thing here, again, is stay calm. Get the facts. Take whatever actions you possibly can. Make adjustments.

As the Marine Corps says, adjust, adapt, respond. Whenever you have an emergency, adjust, adapt, respond. Take whatever action you possibly can, but mostly stay calm.

Dan

Brian, again I'd like to ask you, if there were only one thing you had to say to people about what to do when life throws you a curveball, what would that be?

Brian

The most important thing is to expect to have setbacks and difficulties throughout your life. One subject that I teach—and I've studied it exhaustively for at least thirty years—is called *crisis anticipation*. In crisis anticipation, you sit down and you say, "What are the worst possible things that can happen to me in the different parts of my life?" Use the 3% rule. The 3% rule says that if there is a 3% possibility of this happening, then you should think about it and plan in case it does.

So think about your health: disability, blindness, heart attack, if I lost my voice, if I were unable to walk, unable to work. You think, what would be the worst thing that could happen, and what would I do if that were to occur?

First of all, you organize your health habits. You do everything possible that you can, but you also make provision with your insurance, with savings, with disability payments, with everything, so if this happens, it's not going to destroy your family. You plan in advance. The mark of the superior person is advanced planning and crisis anticipation.

In your business, what's the worst thing that could happen? Your business could go bankrupt. All right. What would be the first step you could take now to make sure that you are protected against that? Or if you had a major reversal? Build up cash reserves. It's one of the things that they tell you in every business book. Once your business starts to grow, put everything back into it, and build up cash reserves.

Expect there to be dramatic down months. Expect there to be crises or things that will happen. Don't spend every penny you have and end up with an empty bank account in the face of a crisis.

If you're thinking about your family, what's the worst thing that can happen? You buy insurance. You buy safety seats for your young children, and you buy the best seats possible so that if the worst happened, if the car flipped, your child would be safe.

We had a friend whose wife was on the phone once and talking away. Talk, talk, for half an hour. Then she turned around and starting looking for her child. But she'd left the door open to the backyard, where the swimming pool was.

They had a plastic sheet over the Jacuzzi, and this little child, two years old, walked out, and walked around the pool. The child stepped on the plastic sheet and was sucked under the water and was unable to move. The child drowned at the bottom of the Jacuzzi.

It destroyed their lives. It ended up in a divorce, and years later, they're still angry with each other and angry with themselves.

My children were never alone in their lives until they were old enough to drive. We put in higher locks so that they could never get out to the pool. We have grandchildren now, and we have safety locks, kid locks on everything. The kids cannot get into or touch anything where there may be any danger at all.

Why? It only has to go wrong once for a total trauma. Therefore, what are the worst things that could happen with your kids? Guard against them. Don't ever trust to luck.

There's an old saying that hope is not a strategy. Wishing is not a strategy. Trusting to luck is not a strategy. In fact, it's a formula for disaster.

Therefore, always guard against the worst things that could happen. Think them through in advance. Take the steps in advance.

You're taking a trip. You have to be there. I'm a professional speaker. You never take the last flight for a speech that you're doing the next day, because what if the last flight cancels or has a mechanical problem?

You can lose the whole talk. All the organizer's time is wasted. You're sitting on one side of the country, and you can't get there. So you always take one or two flights before the last flight.

You always get in early rather than late. You never cut it too close. You always buy time.

The smartest of all people play down the chessboard. Say, "What are the worst things that can possibly go wrong, and if they were to happen, how could I guard against them or minimize the cost?"

NINE

Motivating Others: The Secrets to Servant Leadership

Dan

Brian, we've mostly focused on how we motivate ourselves and how we sustain that motivation throughout our lives. But now we're going to focus on motivating other people, particularly in your job or your business. How do you motivate people to do better? How can you create an environment of motivation for those people?

We've been saying throughout that motivation is an inside job. Thus it might sound like a contradiction in terms to talk about motivating others, but there's no doubt that some leaders, coaches, and parents do a better job of getting others to perform well and to be enthusiastic about doing so. What are some of the essential differences between managers, leaders, coaches, and parents who have highly motivated and high-performing teams and those that don't?

Brian

The most important and most common human desire is to be happy, to have high self-esteem, to feel confident, to feel secure, to feel good about yourself and what you're doing. We talked earlier about feeling like a winner. Really excellent managers, executives, leaders, coaches, teachers, make people feel like winners. And the way to make people feel like winners is to set up a structure that enables them to win.

A perfect example: in a marathon, which is 26.2 miles, they have a mile meter at every mile so that when you are running, you can see it. You can hit the next meter, then the next meter. People win one mile at a time. If they only had one finish line, and you ran for twenty-six miles, three hours, without ever knowing how close or how far away you were, people would lose heart.

There was a famous story about Florence Chadwick, who was the first woman to swim the English Channel. She swam from France to England, to the White Cliffs of Dover—the narrowest part. The first time she tried, she swam, and swam, and swam, and the fog came down. It came down and covered the water, and at about a mile away from her goal, she gave up. She had support boats, and she gave up and had them pull her into a boat.

She said later, "I could have made it if I could have just seen the other side. I didn't realize how close I was, but I just didn't see the other side." So the next time she swam the channel, they made sure that the weather would be clear all day long. She swam the channel, and became the most famous swimmer in history. Even to this day, she set a record.

Well, people need to swim a channel. They need to win. They need to succeed. They did a study which they consider to be perhaps the most profound study in managerial success and business success ever done. It has been reported on now, but it has not been written up. When it's written up, it's going to become one of the most popular management books of all.

They took 22,000 businesses in twenty countries, and they took 150 researchers over ten years, and they analyzed them against many different qualities and characteristics to find out what separated the most profitable companies from the least profitable, the most profitable countries from the least profitable, and the most profitable companies inside a given industry, the top 20%.

They found three things. Actually, three plus one. The first thing they found was that the most successful companies had very clear goals and objectives at every level. Everybody knew exactly what their goal was, what they were expected to accomplish, the results that they were expected to get to help the company to succeed. And they spent a lot of time talking about their goals, clarifying them, so everybody knew. In other words, they knew where the finish line was.

Number two was they had very clear measures and standards and benchmarks. Every single job, and every part of every job, was measured, and there was a number attached to it, so that a person always knew how close or how far away they were from achieving their goal—like the marathon runner.

The third factor was schedules and deadlines. Each person knew exactly what they needed to achieve and how it would be measured, and when it was expected to be accomplished. In other words, the very best companies set up everyone to be a winner. Every single person knew what they had to do to win. They knew exactly what it was, and they did it.

Now I said it was three plus one. The fourth was very high rewards for excellent performance, and this is called a *performance culture*. If a person not only meets, but exceeds, the expected quotas and standards, they get a bonus. If they do a good job, they get a great bonus.

Jack Welch became president of General Electric and managed it for twenty years. He took it from $5 billion in sales to $160 billion—one of the most profitable and successful companies in history. Soon after he began, he installed a performance culture. In this performance culture, a top executive earning $500,000 a year to run a major division could earn $500,000 or a $1 million bonus at the end of the year by exceeding expectations, by exceeding the expected accomplishments. So everybody in that company, including and especially the very best people, was just flaming every day to hit those numbers. To exceed the numbers.

They had four levels of accomplishment. The first was Average: that you had completed your job and everyone was happy. The second level was Excellent: that you had actually done your job at an excellent level and it was recognized by people, and for that, you got a bonus—maybe 10% or 20% of your salary. The third level they had was Wow. At Wow, you got double your salary. And then they had Double Wow, and at Double Wow you got triple your salary.

Everybody in that company thought in terms of Wow and Double Wow. Everybody wanted to win, and win big. This company was in the paper almost every day as one of the fastest growing, most innovative, highest profit industry movers and shakers, and it was because all of these people had this Wow/Double Wow mentality.

So a really good leader structures the work so that people can win all the time. Every job, even small jobs, are very clear and they're measureable, and they have a deadline or a timeline to them.

Now the next thing: in the Olympics and in great races, they find that the greatest world records are set in front of the biggest audiences. In other words, you can't just run and come across the finish line; you've got to have the cheering of the crowds. So the executive, the manager, becomes the cheerleader. He praises and encourages and rewards and makes it a big thing when people hit their targets. Even if they're hitting little targets, as I said before, even if they just get the first deployment with the decisionmaker that's going to lead to a sale in seven months, they make a big thing of it.

The manager takes the person out for lunch, mentions it at the staff meeting, and leads a hand of applause. "So and so did this last week, and boy, it was really hard. We know how tough it is out there. Let's give him or her a round of applause."

Everybody loves to applaud their fellow workers, and while they're doing it, they're thinking, "I want to be the person who gets applause next time." The person who gets the applause can hardly wait to call home and tell his wife or her husband, "Hey, you won't believe what happened to me today." They remember that hand of applause and the praise and the encouragement that they got from the company. They remember it for months. It just shines.

So you think, "Well, this is pretty simple stuff." Yes, it is. And the best companies and the best leaders do it. This is the starting point of servant leadership, which we'll talk about shortly. It's to make people feel important. Make them feel valuable. Make them feel worthwhile. Make them feel that they are making a vital contribution to the company. This comes from you. It comes from the way you treat people.

A couple of years ago, I wrote a top-selling book called *Full Engagement*. It was based on the fact that 65–67% of employees today do not feel fully engaged with or committed to their companies. In fact, they are looking out at the corner of their eye for a better job with another company, should it come along. I said, "Here are the things that you do to create an environment where people are fully engaged, they love to come to work, and they hate to leave the office. When they do leave, they leave with their coworkers, and they go with their coworkers to the bar or the restaurant, and they talk about the work and the business." They are totally engaged. Those businesses are two or three times as productive, dollar for dollar, as the companies where people just go to work, do their jobs, leave at 5:00, and don't think about it afterwards.

Dan

Let's talk about how great leaders help others motivate themselves by creating an environment where motivation, creativity, and high performance can flourish. Specifically, culture. My mom was a principal of a high school that had a great culture, and it was a unique culture among Catholic high schools in the Chicago area. That's the secret, I think, of any great organization: there's a dynamic culture. It's not something another school or another organization can import instantly. It takes a while to develop that. What are some of the essentials for fostering an environment of full engagement?

What things should people put into the environment that surrounds their workers, or their kids, that allow them to shine?

Brian

Some years ago, I was invited to speak for one of the biggest companies on the world. They said, "Before you speak to our managers, you should know what they have been trained in. Here is the workbook." It was numbered and categorized as Top Secret. "We will allow you to read this over the weekend," they said, "but you are not allowed to take notes or photocopy it or duplicate it in any way. And you need to give it back on Monday."

So I sat down with this management program. It was about 300 pages, and I spent all day Saturday and all day Sunday with it. This company had fanned out worldwide and studied 120 teams in their worldwide operation that had accomplished extraordinary things: reduced the costs of a highly competitive product by 80%; speeded time to market to six months rather than one year; dramatically increased sales and profitability by 300% or 400% or 500%. These divisions were exemplary.

They hired a company to go in and determine the common denominators of these winning teams and put them together into this extensive program, and teach this formula for success to every up-and-coming executive in the company. I was so impressed when I read this that I went back and said, "I would love to be able to teach this to my business audiences." They said, "No, this is top secret. We spent a fortune figuring these things out." And I said, "What could I do to go around this?" They said, "You could write a letter to the president."

So I wrote a letter to the president of this company, and I got a reply back giving me permission to teach these ideas. Not the whole process, but the ideas that were essential for business leaders. I'm the only person in the world that has ever been given the permission to teach them.

Here are the five principles in this incredible process. Principle number one was *shared values*. Everybody sits down and talks about culture. Your culture is always based on the values that you have in common. When IBM was established, it started off with three basic values. So with your company, you sit down and you say, what are our values? What do we believe in and stand for? What will we not compromise? The values, as we said earlier, can be fairly simple. They can be things like honesty and integrity, quality products and services, excellent customer service, respect for others, profitability, and so on.

So in the best companies in this study, they found that they would all sit down, and they would vote and come up with a consensus about the three to five core values of their business. They said, "We may change products and services and markets and sales and profits, but we never deviate from these values. Is that agreed?" Everybody agrees. So that's number one. That's the heart, or the core, of culture of a business.

Interestingly, there is a program in America called the Malcolm Baldrige National Quality Award. This was founded by Malcolm Baldrige when he was the Secretary of Commerce under Ronald Reagan. He noticed that there was a special Deming Prize in Japan, which was awarded for the highest quality companies in Japan. W. Edwards Deming was an American who preached the idea of quality control. He was ignored in the '50s and '60s, so he went to Japan and preached his idea there. It transformed the Japanese economy, made it the number three economy in the world. The highest award that you can get in Japan for a company is a Deming Prize.

In the '80s, Baldrige said that we should have something like that in America. So they established the Baldrige Award. The Baldrige Award has a thirty-, forty-page questionnaire that you have to fill out. You have to add $350,000 to cover the costs of all the investigation that they will do. Then they will come, and they'll fan out into your company. They'll talk to your customers, your suppliers, your staff at all levels; they'll talk to your executives; they'll talk to the people in the financial markets, to check to see if this really is a high-quality company.

One question that they ask is, what are the values, the core values, of this business? And here's the rule: they have to be able to ask anybody at any level of the company, and the person can respond immediately. They could be interviewing a janitor on the loading dock and ask, "What are the core values of this company?" The janitor should be able to stand up and say, "Our core values are truth, integrity, quality service, and respect for the individual." If they ask anyone in the company and that person does not know the values, they tear up your application and keep the $350,000, because you are obviously not a quality company. That was the starting point.

So number one is shared values. Number two is *shared goals and objectives*. They would sit down and everybody would talk about, and plan, and agree on, their goals and what they were—how they would be measured, when they were due, and what would be required of everyone to achieve them.

Number three was *shared plans of action*. They would all agree on who was going to do what and when and to what standard, and they were all committed to fulfilling their responsibility. Everybody agreed that they would all fulfill their responsibilities and that everybody would know what everyone else was doing.

Step number four was *continuous review of performance*, both internal and external. They would sit down with each other and they would say, "How are we doing? How is everything going?" They were always open. They would say, "You didn't do this, and you said you would have this done." Everything was done openly and above board. There was no politics, there were no cliques. If somebody said they were going to do it, they would do it.

Number five was called *leading by example*. The head of the team was what they called the orchestra conductor type of leader. Not like the coach, who shouts at people to run the ball. Not like the military officer, who gives people orders. Not like the professor, who operates on a consensual basis with his peers. The leaders would lead the action and saw themselves as the facilitators. Their job was to make it possible for everyone else to do their job. They would ask them, "What do you need to do your job? Do you need extra equipment or people or resources? Do you need time? Do you need funds to be able to travel?" The manager saw himself as the leader who made it possible for everyone else to do their work.

I have trained companies all over the world with these five principles, and it's quite astonishing. They come back and they say, "We've revolutionized our business. We thought everybody knew the values, but when we sat down, nobody was clear. We thought that everybody knew what our goals and objectives were, but when we asked people to be specific, nobody could say. They all had their own different versions."

Here's an example that I give in my seminars. I say there is a Law of Three in the world of work. This law says that there are three things that you do that contribute 90% of your value in your work; everything else you do is in the other 10%. Therefore one of the great keys to success is to do the Big Three.

The way that you determine the Big Three is you say, if you could only do one thing for your business all day long, which would be the most important thing that you could do? What would make the greatest contribution? I have people think about that and write it down. And I say, "All right, now imagine you could only do two things all day long. What would be the second biggest contributor of value to your business and to yourself?" That takes a little bit more time. And then I say, "If you could only do three things all day long, what would be number three?"

This exercise takes about ten to fifteen minutes, until people are clear. I say, "Now the next thing you need to do is check with your boss and your coworkers and make sure that your idea is consistent with theirs." Many managers will go back and say, "These are my Big Three," and the people around them will say, "No, they're not. That's not your job at all. *This* is your job." Your boss will say, for example, "The most important thing you should be doing is meeting with our key clients on a regular basis, face-to-face, but it's not even on your list."

So get clear about your Big Three. And everybody nods and agrees that this is a great idea. Then I'll say to the managers, "Now I would like to invite you to play a game with me, and the game is called Keep Your Job. Before you agree to play with me, let me tell you the rules, OK?" And I say, "Here are the rules. I'm going to ask you to write down the names of the people who report to you—your subordinates, your staff, your team—and I'm going to ask you to write down next to those names the three most important things that they can do to make the most valuable contribution in their work. You'll write this all down, and then I'm going to take your list while you sit here. I'm going to talk to your employees, and I'm going to ask them what the three most important things are that they do in their work here. If their answers and your answers are the same, you get to . . ."

Dan

Keep your job.

Brian

Keep your job. I said, "Does anybody here want to play?" I've done this for tens of thousands of managers. I've never had anyone in the world raise their hand. Nobody wants to play if those are the rules of the game. But the cruelest thing that you can do as a manager is leave people hanging and not knowing the three most important things they could be doing, and in order. The most generous, the most loving, the most positive thing you can do is take the time, all the time, to make sure everybody knows the most important thing that they can do.

I will tell them to do this: "When you get back, have a why-am-I-on-the-payroll? meeting. Have everybody write down the three most important things—their *primary* activities and responsibilities. Then below, you have them write down their three *secondary* responsibilities—the things they do after they've done the Big Three. Then everybody comes to a meeting with photocopies for everyone else. Then you go around, and everybody else discusses everybody's job."

So Julie says, "Well, this is what I think my primary three are, and this is what I think are my secondary three." And everyone looks at these lists, and they discuss her job, and they say, "Yes," or "No, that's not your job, that's *my* job." They find there's overlap, where two people think the same thing is their job. There's under-lap, where nobody thinks it's their job. There's confusion, where people think they're supposed to be doing two totally different jobs. There's contradiction, where if you do one job, you can't do the other job.

You get this all worked out. Everybody comes out of the meeting absolutely clear about their Big Three and their secondary jobs, and they go back to work. The whole business transforms. It's like electricity. Then we say, "All right, how do we measure it, and when is it due?" And we go around and we agree, or sometimes everybody's confused. One person says, "I had no idea that I had to have this done in a week. I didn't know that this had a deadline on it." Other people say, "Of course it's got a deadline. If you don't do that, everything stops in this other area."

Everybody develops our favorite word: *clarity, clarity, clarity.* Once everybody's clear, they are happy and motivated because now you've told them this is how you win. This is how you win, and you can win every day. You can win by starting and completing a little task, starting and completing a big task, starting and completing multiple tasks. It dramatically reduces the amount of chitchat and wasted time and checking email, because you don't get any joy from checking your email, but you do get joy from task completion.

The job of the boss is to make sure that everybody has the resources they need to do their jobs, and then to cheer and applaud. To be the company cheerleader, walking around, telling people how good they are; congratulating people; telling them what a great job they did and how much they're appreciated. This raises the standards, but it also raises morale. It makes people excited about coming to work, because they can start and finish tasks.

Their self-esteem goes up, their self-confidence goes up. Their brains release endorphins, they feel happy and more creative, they are more personable and positive toward other people.

We have thirty people working in my company for my marketing. You walk in, and you'll see everybody is happy. They laugh all the time. They joke all the time. They're smiling. They're busy. They're good friends with each other. They're not wasting time chatting, but they do have meetings at which they talk to each other and share ideas. The spirit in that office is unbelievable, and they are generating more sales and more profits than they ever dreamed possible.

Dan

Brian, there's a type of leadership that's mentioned in the Bible and the *Tao Te Ching*. It's been popularized in recent times by Robert K. Greenleaf. It's called *servant leadership.*

The leader you were just talking about reminds me of this role. The purpose is to serve the employees' highest needs and release their hidden energy and potential, rather than keeping it bottled up, and let the people in the organization grow as a result. You're, again, facilitating.

Discuss, though, how the servant is different from a slave. It's a key difference. Sometimes being a servant to employees means that their needs are best served by enforcing a direction that they may not agree with in the short term, even though it best serves their needs and the organization's. Talk about this key distinction, so people don't think it's a situation where a leader is weak to the point that people are doing their own thing and not following direction.

Brian

Some people try to operate on the basis of democracy and consensus: "Let's all get along, and let's all be friends." They are more concerned with being liked by their coworkers or their employees than they are in getting results.

In studying tens of thousands of businesses, they discovered that the very best management style is called that of the *benevolent dictator.* This expression came out of years of work by William Redding. It refers to a person who is very clear about the results he wants everybody to achieve, but who is still a nice person. He treats people with respect, he always says please and thank you, like your mother told you, but he's very clear that this job has to be done. "This is your job. It has to be done by this time, and I will give you all the help and resources possible, but this is your job and it must be done."

Someone may say, "I've got my kid's soccer game and I was planning to go shopping, and I wanted to pick some—" The benevolent dictator says, "That's fine. You can do that after work, but this job has to be done by this time and to this standard of quality. Are we clear about that? If there's a problem with that, we understand. You can go somewhere else if there's a problem with getting the job done on time."

You see, every breach of discipline leads to breaches of other discipline. Every weakness in dealing with employees leads to the demoralization of everyone else. If I'm working hard to do a good job, but I notice that somebody else can goof off and leave and go to soccer games or go shopping, then I say, "Why am I working my butt off? Why don't I just lean back?"

The person you're letting off the hook becomes weaker and

weaker, because they know that you will never be firm with them. The other people, who are hard workers, become less and less motivated, because they know it doesn't make any difference. You can work yourself silly, and you still get the same rewards as people who are coasting.

In the best companies, everybody knows who the leader is. This is the leader, and the leader is very clear about what needs to be done and the way it needs to be done. They're friendly and supportive, and they give congratulations and thanks, and help, and everything else, but they simply do not relent on the need to get the job done and get it done properly.

It's only then that people can feel like winners. Sometimes people need to be forced to complete their tasks, or they need to be urged or coerced, but it's only then that they can make their full contribution to the company. Then they feel wonderful about themselves, they feel happy, and they laugh.

They did a study of tens of thousands of employees and asked, "Who is the best boss you ever worked for?" The second question they asked was, "Which qualities in this person made him or her the best boss you ever worked for?"

They came up with two qualities. The two C's. The first was *clarity*. "I always knew what my boss expected me to do. It was never ambiguous. He always made it clear what needed to be done, and when and in what order." Number two was *consideration*. "My boss always treated me like I was a person, aside from being an employee. My boss always asked me questions about myself and was concerned about my well-being and my family." So those two: clarity and consideration. Being crystal clear about what needs to be done, and then being a friendly, helpful, and supportive person, and caring about your staff.

Dan

Are there some well-known leaders that you think are good examples of this benevolent dictator approach?

Brian

Well, of course. Executives like Jack Welch. They said that Andrew Grove was one of the toughest people to work for within the entire industry. He cut no corners. He told you straight what he thought. People enjoyed working for this man because he brought out the best in them. There was no nonsense. He would chop you to pieces if you had not done your homework, done your research, if you didn't complete your tasks—and people said they grew more and became more competent, were happier working for Andrew Grove than in any other job they ever had. And they said, "Boy, but he was a bastard to work with."

The critical thing was he set things up so they were always winning. And he insisted that they win. He drove them to get results beyond anything they'd ever done, so they won, and then he would be full of praise; he'd give them bonuses and everything else.

One of the great leaders today, surprisingly, is Mark Zuckerberg of Facebook. Mark Zuckerberg is about thirty-two years old, one of the richest men in the world. Phenomenal story. Mark has a 5:1 question to answer ratio. He's always asking questions. He doesn't talk, he doesn't preach, he doesn't say, "Do this," or lecture, but he's always asking questions, and you better have the answers. He will ask another question, and a follow-up question, and another follow-up question. He will help people become clearer and clearer about who they are, what their job is, and what they are expected to do.

Today Zuckerberg is breaking new ground in a whole series of other fields. He's taking his incredible wealth, the incredible money that Facebook has, and he's invested it in new initiatives to help people to speed things up, to improve communications, and he's involving hundreds and thousands of people in this procedure. And everybody who works at Facebook is absolutely wired, like the people who work at Apple, the people who work at Microsoft, the people who work at Google.

Google is consistently considered to be one of the best companies in the world to work for. Not because you sit around and do nothing, but because everybody is focused on getting results. When you get results, you feel great. When you get results, your coworkers respect you, and you get promoted and you get paid more. When you say, "I work at Google," it's one of the highest accreditations you can have, because Google sets such high standards. If he works at Google, he must be really good—or at Apple, or any one of these companies.

So good bosses have high standards. They insist that people complete their tasks on time. They give them rewards; they give them praise; they give them approbation; they give them time off and ping-pong games and free food, but it's all tied to getting the job done so you can feel like a winner.

Dan

Today we're in a world that is very different from the world of twenty-five years ago when it comes to the structure of the workplace and work hours. People have much more flex time, or they're working at home. There are different types of workplaces. You spoke of Google, which has couches and very open work stations that wouldn't work for other companies.

There's a lot of discussion about Millennials being types that don't like the structured workplaces that were popular during the era of the Baby Boomers. There's all this change going around. How flexible do you think a leader should be in shaping workplace policies and environment? Should any of that really matter? Or is it in the end, as you said, all about results? As long as the results are there, don't worry about the window dressing?

Brian

Many companies now are allowing people to choose their own hours, but these are high-trust companies. These are companies where the people have been selected very carefully, and they've had a chance to perform. And so a lot of people choose their own hours. Want to come in early and work? Some people want to come in at, say, 6:00 and leave at 4:00, to pick up their kids. Do you want to work late? Do you want to be leaving during the day to get something done, and come back and work until 8:00 or 9:00 at night?

But here's the key: you can only do this with high-responsibility employees—and by the way, about 90% of your employees will be high-responsibility if you interview them and select them carefully. There are 10% whom you simply cannot give this kind of freedom to, because they'll abuse it. So you weed them out quickly.

I was talking about my company, with thirty people. If somebody doesn't fit in and doesn't have that attitude of high responsibility—get your job done, whatever time it takes, week-ends or evenings, and so on—get rid of them quickly, because they're like a rotten apple in the bunch. The rule is that everybody knows everything. If you have one rotten apple, everybody knows that this person is not carrying their load.

So good companies sort them out quickly. We say hire slowly, fire fast. And, with regard to Millennials, with regard to Generation X, and so on, they want to be more involved in their work. What does this mean? Just go back to the Big Five.

Number one is shared values. Everyone knows what the organization stands for and believes in, and they buy into the values. If they don't buy in or agree wholeheartedly with ideals such as honesty, integrity, respect for individuals, quality, and service, then this is the wrong place for them. And it's not like, "Well, OK, I'll go along with it." Either you're in, fully engaged, or not at all.

The second is shared goals and objectives, and these are discussed. They're not announced by a boss, like in the old days. They sit down and say, "Look, this is what we need to get done. This is the overall goal. These are the different parts of the goal. How do you think we should go about achieving this goal?" Everybody is fully engaged.

Here's one of the great management concepts: people are committed to the work to the degree to which they have a chance to discuss it. If you announce the job and say, "Please do this," their commitment is very low. It's not even *their* job, it's *your* job. They're helping you out. If you say, "This job needs to be done; how do you think we should approach it? What do you suggest that we do to handle it?" You involve them in a discussion. When they walk away, you have now transferred ownership of the job from you to them. They will then take total responsibility so as not to disappoint you.

The third is a shared plan of action. People are always talking together about what they're doing and what they're doing relative to you, so everybody knows what everyone's job is, and they're constantly clearing up overlaps and underlaps. So everybody is clear about their specific job and how it will be measured and when it needs to be done. Then they have constant evaluation of their products, their services, the way they're working together, the teams, meetings. They're constantly saying, "How are we doing?"

Finally, the leaders lead the action. The leaders go forward. The leaders accept responsibility for setting the example, for being the role models, and for helping other people. They go around all the time and say, "How can I help you? Do you need anything? How is everything going? Are you feeling overloaded? Can you use some help to take some of the work away? Maybe we gave you too many tasks to be done in too short a time." They're constantly out there, managerially massaging all their people so everybody is happy. Everybody feels part of a great team. Everybody feels listened to. Everybody feels as though they're participating.

The two most important qualities of great companies, according to the website A Great Place to Work: number one is trust. There's a very high level of trust in the workplace. Everybody trusts each other, and as a result they're spontaneous, they're happy, and they share ideas. Number two is everybody feels in the know. They feel that they're always kept up-to-date. They know everything that's going on in the business. There are no secrets, no closed doors. There are no cliques. There's no confidential stuff. Everything is wide open. These are the two most important things that a manager can bring to a workplace for workers at any level, but especially for the Millennials and Generation X.

Dan

Is there a final key insight you wanted to leave with people on effective leadership?

Brian

Perhaps the most important thing I ever learned about leadership was from Drucker, again, and he was asked, are leaders born or are they made? He said, "There may be born leaders, but they are so few that they make no difference in the great scheme of things. Leaders are made. Leaders are self-made. They are self-made by work on themselves, and every person can develop themselves into becoming a leader. A leader is a person who accepts responsibility for results. If you accept responsibility for results, you can become a leader with no followers. But if you accept responsibility for results, and you get the results that people are depending upon, you will soon have other people working with you to help you to get more and more results. You job is to become a multiplication sign so that you get great results. Then, when you are given assistants to work with you, working with them, you get more and more results."

Many years ago, I mentioned earlier, I worked for a man who started at the bottom of an international company. He became so good at working with other people that he was given an assistant, and then a second assistant. When I worked with him, he had a staff of 10,000 under him, and they all said, "This the best boss I ever had in my life."

TEN

Beyond Motivation: The Power of Rituals for Living an Extraordinary Life

Dan

Brian, we've come to the end of our journey, and to probably one of the most important parts of our program. There are some subjects in which a sign of success is being able to transcend or let go of that very subject at some point.

For example, I think the sign of a successful parent is one who raises such independent, motivated, and happy children that the children can then lead themselves, and the parent's role eventually becomes unnecessary. Whereas the unsuccessful parent is one who raises a dependent and unmotivated child, who ends up depending on the parent well into early adulthood and perpetuating that parent role.

It can also be said that a good primary care doctor is one who educates and informs his patients to be proactive about their own health in order to avoid major health issues in the future. In essence, he is helping them to become their own doctor, rather than needing a doctor again and again and again for endless ailments.

I think of motivation as a similar subject. A sign of a successful person is one whose life is fine-tuned to the point where it's set up to succeed, so that eventually constant motivation to succeed day after day is almost unnecessary. One achieves this by setting up one's life with a daily set of rituals or habits that make it possible to succeed with far less effort. Can you discuss how setting up your life with an empowering set of rituals or habits can make motivation less of an issue?

Brian

Yes. When I began to study time management, some people would say to me, "If you manage your time too tightly, you become too rigid, you're not flexible, you're not spontaneous, you're not enjoyable," and so on. I investigated that idea very carefully, and I found that it's exactly the opposite. The more things in your life that you can make automatic, so that you don't even think about doing them, the more you can free your mind for higher level activities. The more things that are automated, the more you can use your mind to achieve more of your goals, so when you get up in the morning you don't say, "How do I put toothpaste on my toothbrush? How do I make the eggs?" No, you do them unthinkingly, and it frees up your mind for more important things.

Successful people develop rituals that enable them to perform at a far higher level. I gave you my little formula to increase your income 1000%: 2% a month, 25% a year, ten times in ten years. Those are rituals that you go through your daily life. I've had thousands of people come back to me and say, "Once you get into the rhythm of getting up early, rewriting your goals, studying and upgrading your skills, planning your day in advance, and so on, you get so much more done with so little stress that you look forward to doing it. It becomes automatic and easy."

My recent book is on the power of habit. It's very hard to develop a habit initially, but then it's very easy to live with. It's very difficult to discipline yourself over and over again, but then it locks in and it becomes automatic. You just do it without thinking about it.

Successful people have success rituals. First of all, going to bed time, getting up time. As we said before, your ability to thoroughly rest your mind, your brain, and your body has an incredible effect on your whole day. Remember, you are a thinking machine. All day long you solve problems and make decisions. One great idea is enough to make you rich. One great decision can transform a business. One problem solved can enable you to make more progress in a couple of years than many people make in many years.

So, first of all, go to bed early, get up early. You've heard it said from Benjamin Franklin, "Early to bed and early to rise makes a man healthy, wealthy, and wise." The only reason we don't go to bed early is that we get distracted by television, so the rule is turn off the television by 9:00 so that your brain can unwind, and go to bed at 10:00. They've found in a recent study that rich people watch less than one hour of television a day, and they usually watch it prerecorded so they can watch it on their own schedule. If you watch television before you go to bed, it can get your mind all scrambled up.

Another thing: you should eat three hours before bedtime, because that enables the food to digest, and it enables you to fall asleep. If you eat any closer to sleep, it can keep you awake and give you bad sleep, so you're in bed for the same number of hours but you wake up tired out, you wake up dragging yourself. So be very alert and jealous about getting enough sleep: think about it, plan it, organize it, put other things aside.

I have some good friends, who are very successful. When we were younger, we would go out for dinner at 8:00 or 9:00, eat and drink until 10:00 or 11:00, and go home at midnight. He and his wife now eat dinner at 5:00 or 6:00, and they go to bed at 8:00, or 9:00 at the very latest. They get up at 4:00 or 5:00, and they work, and they have a tremendously productive working day. If you get eight, nine, even ten hours of sleep at night, you are much more productive the following day. So make it a ritual to go to bed early and get up early.

I always advocate making a list of everything you have to do the next day the night before. Go over your list and organize it and have it in your mind. One of the main reasons we don't go to sleep is that we stay awake tossing and turning, thinking about something that we have to do tomorrow that we forgot to write down. When you write down everything, it clears your mind completely. It's almost like clearing off one of those magic white slates. Your mind is completely clear, because everything you have to do tomorrow is written down.

Writing things down also taps into the powers of your mind. Your subconscious mind and your superconscious will work on that list all night. Often when you wake up in the morning, you'll have a perfect insight, or a perfect idea, about how to solve a problem or achieve a goal. So you write down your goals for the day the night before, and all night this incredible subconscious computer is working to bring you ideas. Many of the greatest breakthroughs in life happen to people who have woken up, sometimes in the middle of the night, with an idea that's changed their lives. Some of the great scientific breakthroughs took place as a result of this.

By the way, always have a pad of paper and a pencil or pen on your nightstand, so, if you wake up in the night with a great idea, you can write it down, because if you don't, it will disappear. There's a rule from Napoleon Hill: "Catch the idea and write it down." Imagine the idea is flying through the air like a comet. Catch the idea and write it down. Sometimes that idea will change your life.

A second ritual, which I practice every day, is exercise when you get up in the morning. I had this discussion recently with professional physiotherapists. Over and over they say that if you are a morning exerciser, you're much more likely to stay at it, and you're much more likely to get all the benefit of exercising. If you make a decision to exercise later in the day, you're much more likely to make excuses. You're tired. You're busy. It's late. So I get up in the morning and I immediately exercise for fifteen to fifty minutes. At the very least, I will do a whole series of stretching exercises, sit-ups, core exercises.

By the way, every person should do between 100 and 200 sit-ups every morning. This is the one muscle you can't wear out. The way you do these—I learned this from an athletic specialist—is you put your hands behind your head and you pull your knees up with your feet flat on the floor, and you just raise your shoulders. You don't go any further than that. You don't have to do these Marine sit-ups, where you're crunching and so on. All you have to do is get your shoulders off the floor so they tighten up your muscles, and you can do that 100 times. Almost anyone can do that ten, twenty, fifty, 100 times. When you exercise your core, you strengthen your whole body and your posture, you feel better, and you have fewer pains in your back, in your hips, in your knees, in your shoulders. Just that little exercise.

My favorite exercise is called a wig-wag. You lie on the floor on your back and you pull your knees up, and your feet are flat on the floor. Then you turn your knees to as far as possible to one side and your head to the other, and then to the one side, and your head to the other. I do that thirty times, and then I do 150 to 200 sit-ups, and then I do the wig-wag 30 times more.

This completely exercises your full spine, from your neck to your coccyx. Your whole spine is being rotated sixty times every day. It's completely noninvasive. It takes no muscular strength. But it's one of the greatest guarantors that you'll never have back problems. Today back problems are experienced by 50% of people past the age of forty. It's because they don't continually rotate their spines.

The other thing I do is aerobic exercise, which is absolutely essential. If you do aerobic exercises in the morning, you are brighter, sharper, more creative, and you have more energy all day long. I have my own treadmill, my own elliptical machine, and my own exercise bicycle. Plus I have a pool across the street at the country club, which has 72 feet per lap, so you can go over there and swim a tenth of a mile, a quarter of a mile, a half a mile, a mile.

So you need about 200–300 minutes of exercise each week, and you plan it the same way you would plan a business meeting. "This morning I get up and I do this set of exercises," and then maybe you add on aerobic exercises. "I swim twice a week, half a mile a swim, one mile a week. I set the date, I set the time, and I get up in the morning, and I go and do it."

I joke with my wife that I wake up at 6:00 or 6:30, I grab myself by the scruff of the neck, and I take myself and throw myself into the pool before I know what's happening, and then I just thrash back and forth. This keeps you pumped all day long.

If you exercise on a regular basis, you start to inject endorphins, "nature's happy drug," into your blood and your brain. If you take any drug repeatedly, eventually you develop an addiction. And the finest addiction you can develop is to endorphins, because you can only get endorphins when you do something that is life-enhancing. When you laugh, when you love, when you read something that you enjoy, when you write your goals, when you walk, and especially when you do aerobic exercise, you activate these endorphins, and you feel good for hours. If you do this repeatedly, soon you become addicted to getting up in the morning and exercising. Soon you have to resist the temptation to do it, because you start to look forward to how good you're going to feel afterwards.

Another ritual for success is to meditate for fifteen minutes every day. I find meditation is not easy for me, but spiritual reading, solitude, and contemplation of what I'm reading is very enjoyable. So you can do any of those four things. You can meditate if you like. But here's the danger with meditation: 50–70% of meditators just fall back to sleep. They get up in the morning, and they meditate and just fall asleep. They've tracked this at Harvard. "I'm meditating." No, you're not. You just went back to sleep; you got fifteen minutes more sleep.

But if you get up and do your exercises, it gets you stimulated. Then you take something that is either educational, or motivational, or spiritual—a single chapter in a book will do it—and you sit there and read it and think about how you could apply it to your day. There's a rule from a great preacher named Henry Drummond. He said, "The first hour is the rudder of the day." Whatever you put into your mind mentally in the first hour sets you up for the whole day. This is why you must avoid reading the news, and all the garbage about the rapes, the murders, and the corruption, first thing in the morning, because that's what sets you up for negativity.

Read something that's positive and uplifting for the first fifteen minutes to thirty minutes each day, and then you can do something else. I like to start the day after I've exercised with a cup of coffee. You combine a cup of coffee with reading something uplifting, underlining—never read without a pen in your hand so that you can underline—and you wake up, and it's almost as if you've taken a spiritual pill. You feel happy. You feel ready for the day. And you're far more creative.

Write down six priorities each day. My rule is to buy yourself a spiral notebook; it costs about $1.50. If you can't afford it, your mother will give you the money, because she wants you out of the house anyway. Open it up, and write today's date and place, and write down ten goals, as we talked about before, in the present tense. You can write down more than ten, but you must write down ten every day.

I used to offer a coaching program, and I would guarantee that if you came to me one day every three months and went through one solid day of exercises with me in planning, productivity, focus, concentration, and so on, you would double your income *and* double your time off in one year. If you didn't, I would give you your money back. There will be no charge for the year. I never had a request for a refund.

In my coaching program, I always front-loaded the first day with a series of ideas that would be guaranteed to double people's incomes. First I'd have everybody write down ten goals. Then I would hand out a spiral notebook, and I would say, "This is going to be your new best friend. For the next thirty days I'm going to ask you to do just this one thing. Open this up every morning and write down your ten goals without reference to what you wrote yesterday. You're not copying your ten goals. You're starting over again with a clean page by memory. And the most remarkable thing is going to happen. Some of the goals you wrote down during the first exercise will fall off the list. You'll forget to rewrite them because they're not that important. Other goals will move up the list, and you will write them with even greater clarity. Other goals will move down. You'll start to rephrase the goals, develop new goals, and suddenly you'll start to achieve them."

One of my students did this exercise with me on a Friday, and by Thursday of the next week he had accomplished five of his ten goals for the year. He said he could not believe it. It was like pushing down on a dynamite detonator. Everything exploded—business goals, life goals, family goals, friendship goals, money goals. It just started to happen at an incredible rate. He said, "I achieved more in one week with those ten written goals than I expected to achieve in a year or two."

So just do it. I would say to my students, "Do it every day for a month. It takes three minutes to five minutes to write down your ten goals. Just do it for one month and see what happens." I've had countless people say they've paid tens of thousands of dollars for coaching programs, and they made more progress with this one idea than with three years of courses and coaching and classes.

Try it out. Your whole life will begin to change. From then on, if it works, do this every morning as a ritual: get up, do your exercise, do your spiritual reading, write down your ten goals. That list of ten goals sets you up for the day. It activates your subconscious and superconscious. It activates your reticular cortex, which is the device in your brain that causes you to start to notice things that you hadn't noticed before. If you write down "I want to drive a brand new Mercedes-Benz, black, silver, four-door, with leather upholstery," from that moment on you're going to see black Mercedes everywhere, and you're going to see different things that you can do to acquire the funds that you need to buy the car.

Another ritual has to do with email. Don't check your email in the morning: your email, as we said, is a dessert activity. So resist the temptation to get up in the morning and check your email. There are people who have become so addicted to email that they get up in the night and they check their email. They even leave their cell phone on so it rings and wakes them—and usually whomever they're with—throughout the night. They don't want to miss anything.

Why is this? We talked about addiction before. In email, whenever a bing goes off, a bing, something new, unexpected, it's like a slot machine. It triggers a shot of dopamine across your brain. It's just like an electrical shock, or a distant piece of lightning that goes across the sky. A little bit of dopamine shoots across your brain, and it's a stimulant. Dopamine is the same stimulant that is in cocaine and other bad drugs, and it stimulates you, it alerts you, it gives you energy, makes you curious, makes you jump, so you immediately check your email.

That's why people leave their email and their phones on all day. Whenever they go off, it gives them a jolt, and they have to check. If they get low on jolts, they send out emails to their friends, who reply to them, and they get a jolt back. So what happens after you check your first email in the morning is you get addicted to dopamine.

With alcoholism they say, "One drink is too many, and no number is enough." If you're an alcoholic, you cannot drink one drink. That's the reason they have Alcoholics Anonymous meetings at drinking time—7:00 in the evening. You meet with your group, and you stay there for two hours or three hours talking, and chatting, until the major drinking time, the habitual time for having a drink after work, has passed. Then you go home and maybe you'll be OK. But if you have one drink, you cannot stop drinking until you pass out. Anybody who knows about alcoholics knows this.

It's the same thing with dopamine. Once you get your first shot of dopamine, you cannot stop checking your email all day long. The average adult today checks their email 145 times a day. The average college student checks their email and their Facebook eighteen times an hour. They usually move while they're hooked up to their phone, so they've got earphones. It may be off so that other people can't hear it, but they can hear every bing, every blip, every ring. They have different rings for different people, so they know, "Oh, that's Susan calling me." "Oh, that's an assignment." They're being jolted all the time. As a result they can't concentrate.

Dopamine is the anticoncentration drug. As I said before, all success in life comes from task completion. All success in life comes from taking an important task and concentrating single-mindedly on that task until it's complete. If you want to be rich and successful, start with your most important task every morning, and stay with it until it's complete before you do anything else. If you can discipline yourself to work flat out for ninety minutes each morning, and then ninety minutes more, and complete one major task, your whole life will change. You'll engage in neuroplasticity. You'll reshape and reform the channels of your brain. You'll develop whole new ways of acting and thinking through repetition.

The great breakthrough in neuroscience in the last ten years is that your brain is infinitely plastic, really until the eighth or ninth decade of life. If you start to feed yourself with new information, it starts to develop new neural channels, and you begin to think, and respond, and act differently. You can transform your life by doing things repeatedly. But if you start checking your email first thing in the morning, pretty soon it becomes easier and easier and less and less resistible. You cannot stop checking your email.

The best time managers—and they've done some studies at Harvard on this too—say that many managers' careers are being ruined by an obsession with email. Now they have coaches and counselors that work with executives in Fortune 500 companies that sit there and say, "Stop it. Don't do it. Put it away." At first they're like drunks—they just keep reaching, almost spasmodically, for their iPhones, or checking their email. Turn it off, shut it down, leave it off. One great rule is from Thomas Moore, the philosopher and author of *Care of the Soul,* is leave things off. Leave off the television. Leave off the computer. Leave off the iPhone. Leave things off and create silence.

Tim Ferriss wrote one of the best books out there. It's called *The Four-Hour Work Week,* when he started off he was working fourteen hours a day, seven days a week, checking, answering emails. By the time he finished, he was checking his emails once a week, and he'd tripled his income. He takes three months or four months of vacation each year, he travels around the world, he's learned new subjects and new languages, he's never made more money in his life, and he checks his email once a week.

He explains the process of setting up a virtual assistant or an executive assistant. He has a virtual assistant in the Philippines, and all his emails go to her. He has a list of frequently asked questions, so if people write and ask one of these, she just plugs in the answer. If it's an emergency, then she sends it on to him, wherever he happens to be in the world. And he said that over time there have been fewer and fewer emergencies—maybe once a week—that his virtual assistant can't handle. He's making more money than he's ever made in his life, and he's checking his email once a week. Just think about that.

People say, "I can't do that." Well, I'm flying from Los Angeles to Frankfurt tomorrow. I will be in airplanes for fifteen hours. I will not be able to check my email for fifteen hours. And you know something? The world will continue to turn. Nothing will happen. Everything will be just fine.

Eat a nutritious breakfast. There's a wonderful expression, "Well begun is half done." Your mother told you that breakfast is the most important meal of the day, because the food that you eat in the morning gives you the energy that you need to run your life. It's almost like starting off on a trip with an empty tank of gas. When you wake up in the morning, your tank is empty; your glucose levels are low. So you have to fill your tank, and what you fill your tank with largely determines the quality of your day.

Some years ago a man named Barry Sears wrote a book called *The Zone*. It became one of the best-selling books on diet in history, and it's life-transforming. He said that every food you take is a chemical. Every chemical has side effects. If you drink a Coke or a Red Bull, or eat toast, or bacon, these have side effects. So eat the foods that are the most perfectly balanced to give you the highest level of energy for the longest period of time. These are proteins. So in the morning you eat eggs, but you don't eat toast or bagels.

One rule for success is eliminate the three white poisons: sugar, flour, and salt. The average American consumes something like twenty or thirty pounds of salt in their diet each year, and they need none. They take in salt in candies, and in Cokes. One can of Coke, by the way, has twelve tablespoons of sugar. We have an obesity epidemic because people are drinking these huge glasses of soft drinks. One of those big Slurpees that you get may have almost a cup of sugar in it. Of course the sugar builds up and builds up. So you have a 36% obesity rate in America today. We are the fattest people in the world. In fact, an expression came out of Harvard: *Porcus Americanus.* When I go to Europe, I've started to talk about a proper diet, but there are no fat people in the audience. And I say, "I think I'll just pass over this one. It's not necessary for you to hear."

Start off with a high protein diet, which is eggs, and complex carbohydrates, which means fruits and vegetables. That will give you enough food energy to run for five straight hours. At lunchtime, eat salads with protein. Don't eat salads with any carbohydrates, no breads, no pastries, no cakes, no Cokes, no anything else—salad with protein. It can be salad with fish, salad with steak, salad with chicken, or, if you're a vegetarian, even with tofu. That will give you five hours more of high energy and no afternoon drowsiness.

People go into an afternoon slump. In the southern countries they have a siesta. They sleep for two hours, because they eat huge pasta, bean, tortilla lunches. But if you have only protein and complex carbohydrates, fruits and vegetables, for breakfast and lunch, you will have high levels of energy, your glycemic index will be high, and your brain will be functioning at maximum all day long.

If you get into the habit of doing that, you will produce twice as much as the person next to you who comes back from lunch drowsy, having had a heavy meal, and whose brain is half-functioning or malfunctioning. Many companies now are developing sleeping rooms so when people come back from lunch after an hour they can go and sleep, because they're useless anyway. They're just so tired out.

Next, we just talked about a low carb diet. Barry Sears found that if you mix in foods—a carbohydrate like bread, pastry, pasta, rice, even potatoes—with a protein, the carbohydrate causes your body to release alkalines to break it down, and the protein causes your body to release acids to break it down. So now you have a lunch that has proteins and carbohydrates, and your body rushes alkalines and acids into your stomach to break them down.

Now what did we learn in first year chemistry? An acid and an alkaline neutralize each other. So the digestive process stops. Your body goes into a form of emergency and says, we've got to get more blood in there, we've got to start rushing more blood to the stomach to break down this food. You start to burp, and you feel bloated, and the blood is rushed away from your main muscles, your legs and your upper body, and from your brain. You start to feel drowsy and dumb.

That's why they tell you never go swimming an hour after eating. It's because the digestive process is pulling blood away from your muscles, so you'll have cramps and you can even drown. Therefore, if you just simply discipline yourself to eat more proteins and fresh fruits and vegetables, you'll have high energy all day long. So make that a habit.

Then, at work, focus on your strengths and delegate your weaknesses. One thing that we mentioned earlier, is this concept of the Big Three, the Law of Three. Remember: the Law of Three says there are three things that you do that contribute 90% of your value in your work. One of the great keys to success is to do the Big Three.

I've worked with more than 1000 entrepreneurs, for seven years. I worked with them up close and personal for one full day every three months. Some of them came back two years and three years. Again, I would front-load my program. I'd be darn good and sure that people doubled their income so they didn't ask for their money back. We talked about the ten goals, the other one I front-loaded was this idea of the Big Three, and I would help them work these through.

I had a top executive come through this course. I taught the goals and the Law of Three. It's a full day program, but at 2:00 he got up, took his briefcase, and walked out of the room. I went out and caught him, and I said, "Tom, where are you going?" He said, "I'm done." I said, "I unconditionally guarantee this program." He said, "No, I'm not going to exercise the guarantee. I've got my money's worth. Two life concepts, writing down my goals, picking my most important goal and working on it every day, and practicing the Law of Three. I'll double my income by the end of the month just on those two. I don't need to hear anymore." And he did. He tripled and quadrupled his income, and in the years ahead he became a millionaire and retired early, just by setting clear goals, having one big goal and focusing on the Big Three.

So when you go to work, focus on the Big Three. And ask yourself what your strengths and weaknesses are. Really good people have far more strengths than weaknesses, so one of the most important things you do is you get better and better at your Big Three.

Actually there are three rules with your Big Three tasks. Number one is do fewer things—stop doing things. As we said before, you cannot get your life under control except to the degree to which you stop doing small things. We talked about the A task versus the B task. Stop doing the B task.

Number two is to do the Big Three more of the time. Do them all day long, and don't do anything else but those three until you've exhausted all possibilities, which probably will never happen.

Number three, one of the greatest success skills of all is to get better at your three most important tasks. Getting better is the greatest of all time savers. I worked with people in selling, in management, in leadership, in marketing. I've helped them to identify the three most important things they do, and then to develop a learning program for each of those three. They've literally increased their income ten and twenty times over the next couple of years by focusing on becoming really good at the most important things they do, because the only thing that stands between you and extraordinary accomplishment is additional skills. Resolve to be in the top 10% in each of these three areas, and pay any price, go any distance, make any sacrifice to achieve it.

Here's a good point, by the way. Dr. Anders Ericsson at the University of Florida has put twenty-five years of research into what he calls *elite performance*, and his work's been quoted by lots of people. He's the one who came up with the idea that it takes 7000 hours to achieve elite performance. However, subsequent research proves that if you have a natural talent or ability for a particular skill or field, you can achieve elite performance that's in the top 5% or 10% in a year or two. It doesn't take seven years if you already have a natural ability for it.

They looked at income and socioeconomic mobility, which Edward Banfield at Harvard talked about. They asked, why do some people earn so much more than others? They looked at the top executives of the Fortune 500. Last year these people earned an average of $10.3 million each. The average CEO earns 301 times the average income in their company. They all started off at the beginning of their careers at the same starting line. They started running, like in a marathon, and over the years some people got way, way ahead in the income race. The great majority, 80% or more, stayed in the middle, with average income, and a small percentage fell behind. These are the lower class, and the lower-lower class. They just didn't make it, for whatever reason.

Then they looked at the people who got way ahead. The 80/20 rule holds. Some people got into the top 20%, where they were earning more than people in the bottom 80%. But then there's the top 20% of the top 20%, which is the top 4%. These people were earning something like thirty-two times the average of the people in the bottom 80%. Then they took the top 20% of the top 20% of the top 20%, which is the top 0.4%, and these people were earning over fifty times the average of the people in the bottom 80%. And they all started off at the beginning, so they asked, how did they accomplish this?

They checked these people's work records and their performance reviews over the years from different companies, and they found the key strategy. This strategy is worth this entire program.

When they took their first job, these people were young people, twenty, twenty-one, coming from a good college, a poor college, or no college. When they took their first job, they would go to their boss and they would say, "I really want to be valuable around here. What one skill would help me the most to make the greatest contribution to this business?" The boss would say, "Well, if you were really good at this, or really good at that, that would really increase your value. That would be really helpful to us."

So they would decide on that one skill, like a sniper: one shot, one kill. They would write it down as a goal and say, "I am absolutely excellent at this skill by this date." They would make a list of everything that they could think of that they could do to learn this skill—the books they could read, the courses they could take. Some of them would pay their own fees to travel across country and take these courses. They would take unpaid time off, if they felt that that would give them an edge by studying under an expert for two days or three days. They would listen to audio programs in their car, when they were working, when they were walking. They would watch some of the best programs on YouTube, where experts are talking about their subjects. Some people get up every morning and watch a TED talk by one of the world's great experts. Now there's a whole series of TEDx, or sub-TED Talks, that are available on YouTube as well. This is twenty minutes of time with an expert giving their best ideas on an important subject.

They would focus on learning a single subject until somebody said, "You know, you're really good at that." That would be their signal to move on to the next subject. They would then take the next subject and keep working at that until somebody told them they were good at it. How many hours did they spend on this? They found that the average person spends two hours per night five nights a week. This was my story too. I didn't realize that research would bear it out, but when I was young and single, I never went out to bars. I'd go home and study and read and take notes, because I just love to learn.

I was in Sofia, Bulgaria a couple of weeks ago, and I said,

"Excuse me, I'm new here to Bulgaria. How many hours do you have in a week here?" The audience all stopped and then cracked up laughing. I said, "You have 168 hours. Could you carve off ten of those hours to become one of the highest paid and most successful people in your field? Well, if you do, it's virtually guaranteed." And these 500 CEOs all used the same strategy. They learned one key skill at a time, whether it took them a month, or three months, or a year, or even longer. They would focus on that skill, and read, and learn, and talk, and take advice from people until they mastered it.

Albert Einstein said that, "The greatest power in the universe is compounding." It's growing exponentially, the percentage upon the percentage upon the percentage. In learning skills it's the same thing. If you learn a skill and then you learn another skill, it enables you to use the first skill even better, and probably creates more opportunities for you to use it. If you learn a third skill, it multiplies the first two skills. If you learn a fourth skill and a fifth skill, they start to multiply and compound each other. If you imagine an upside down pyramid, you start at the bottom with the lower peak, and as you learn it starts to spread and expand and expand, and soon these people are earning ten, twenty, fifty times as much as the average person.

Anybody can do this, starting today. Anybody can say, "From now on I'm going to devote two hours a day to learning new skills." You can start off by listening to audio programs on your iPhone on your way to work; you can read for thirty minutes to sixty minutes each morning before you get started; you can watch YouTube videos or TED talks, you can listen and watch documentaries, or read something in the evenings. Just make it a ritual: you're going to spend two hours per day, five days a week.

That will virtually guarantee that you'll be one of the most successful people of your generation.

Dan

And the final ritual?

Brian

The final ritual is to realize that there is no joy in things. There is no joy in money or cars or boats. There's no joy in honors and accolades, because they're gone as soon as the applause stops and the room empties, and you're left standing there alone. I've done seminars where I had 5000 people giving me a standing ovation, and I would wait and soon everybody was gone. You're all alone in a 5000-person auditorium. They've all forgotten about you, and they're thinking about dinner.

There's very little joy in accomplishments, except a fleeting kind. Eighty percent of all of our joy in life comes from our relationships with other people. It comes from our interactions. It comes from talking, and living, and laughing, and being part of their lives, and helping your kids grow up, and seeing them laughing, and doing things for your spouse.

So when you're with your family, be there all the time. When you're at work, work all the time you work, but when you're with your family, be there. Being there means head-to-head, knee-to-knee, face-to-face, heart-to-heart. It means that you are there and you're in their face. You're only with another person when you're eyeball-to-eyeball with that person, not when they're down the hall, or you're in your den and they're cooking, or you're watching television,. It's only when you're face-to-face with the other person that you're truly there.

The most important thing is to ask questions, not to pontificate about what you did during the day. Ask them questions about what they did and how their life is going, and then listen intently to the answers. This is the highest form of relationship: when you take the time to listen, and to ask questions, and be patient with people. The only way that you can increase the value of a relationship is by investing more time in it, and by more time we mean face-to-face time, heart-to-heart time. Turn off the television.

You and I were talking earlier about family dinners. They did some work at Harvard many years ago, before I had my first child, and found that a child's character is formed by the conversation around the family dinner table. It's the most important single variable that determines how that young person will turn out as an adult. I thought, "Whoa," so I've insisted with my children that we all have a family dinner. When they were younger, we would have a family dinner virtually every time I was home. If I wasn't there, if I was traveling, they'd have a family dinner with my wife, and they'd all talk about what they did during the day.

Never allow the television to be on during a family occasion, because people's eyes will always move to the greatest stimulus. It's always the television. So leave it off. If you come in and your family member's there, or comes in, turn off the television. If I'm working on something and one of my family members comes in, I turn it off. Leave everything off. I put what I'm reading aside and focus on them as if I'll never see them again.

Gary Smalley was a great teacher. He was a preacher, and he did one of the first really successful television product sales; it was about relationships. He told this story: "Imagine that you're walking down the street, and you see coming towards you someone that you went to school with ten or twenty years ago. You haven't seen them for ten or twenty years, and you immediately remember all the things you did when you went to school. That was your dear friend. You went out on dates and you went to parties."

The person comes closer, and they see you. You say, "It's you. It's you. Holy smokes." And you hug and say, "Gee, how are you? Where have you been? What are you doing? How's your life? Are you working? Where do you live?" You have this incredibly enthusiastic conversation and maybe arrange to meet later. You walk away and think, "Wow, wasn't that great?" You're smiling to see your old friend from school. Then you go home, and you walk in and say, "What's for dinner? Where's the TV control?"

Gary Smalley's point is this: here's someone that you haven't seen for twenty years, and you might never have seen again in your life, and you're treating them like they're the most important person in the world, when the most important people in the world are the people at home. So when you go home and you meet a family member, look at them and say to yourself, "It's you. Oh my, it's you." You brighten up. You smile. You're happy. You hug them. And you tell them how much you love them. You tell them how happy you are to see them.

I learned that thirty-five years ago, when I had my first child, and I've practiced it with all my family members ever since. Since my older children have gotten married, I practice it with their spouses. I hug them, and I'm happy to see them, and I smile. After they had children—I have five grandchildren—whenever they come in, I treat them like "Oh my, it's you. It's you." I drop everything.

If you do this one little thing—treat each member of your family like, "Wow, it's you" every time you see them again—you're going to have one of the most wonderful lives you can possibly imagine. And everything else will be worthwhile.

Dan

What a prescription for a full life!. Brian, we've come a long journey in this program, and you've packed more value into this program than most people get in ten programs. But as best you can, as we close, provide a summary of what you've been trying to accomplish in this program besides motivation, and leave the reader with some advice as they move on in their journey toward a life of success and happiness and fulfillment.

Brian

I usually end my seminars with what I would call the secrets of success for the twenty-first century, and there are three or four of them. The first one is that your life only becomes better when *you* become better, and there's no limit to how much better you can become. The only limit is your imagination. Since your imagination is unlimited, you're going to become better, and better, and better all your life.

One of the greatest motivations of all, according to all the books, articles, and psychological studies being done today, is the feeling of getting better. People go to a company because they feel they're going to make more progress in their life and career there. People are motivated at a company because they feel they're progressing, they're learning new things, they're accomplishing new things. They will work for less money, because they're happy, they feel like winners every day. Every time you learn and apply something new, you feel like a winner. You feel happy. That's why continuous learning is so important.

The second rule is that it doesn't matter where you're coming from. All that really matters is where you're going. Almost all the unhappiness in the world today comes from people thinking and talking about things in the past that made them mad, or sad, or unhappy. One of the great rules of life is, never worry about something that you can't change. And you cannot change a past event. You can only learn from the event, accept responsibility as much as possible, and move on.

You'll find that leaders, the top 10% of men and women in our society, are intensely future-oriented. They think about the future most of the time. You become what you think about. Leaders think about the future. They think about where they're going. They think about what they want and how to get it. They think about their goals. The very act of thinking about something that you want to be or do, or have, makes you happy. It gives you energy, it makes you more creative, it makes you more personable, and it releases endorphins in your brain. It's all good things.

The third critical principle is that you can learn anything you need to learn in order to achieve any goal that you can set for yourself. When I stumbled across this principle at the age of twenty-three, I was poor, living in a flophouse, with holes in my shoes. I had no money, I had no future and no education, and no experience. I came across this principle and it changed my life forever: *I can learn anything I need to learn.*

Ever since, I've been excited about learning. The more you learn, the more you *can* learn. The more you learn, the smarter you become, because you're activating more of your cells and neurons. You activate those; they connect with others. The cells that fire together wire together. The more you fire your cells by learning new things, the more you wire your brain, so you become smarter and smarter and smarter.

Usually the only thing that stands between where you are today and where you want to be is the development of a new skill. Sometimes I'll ask my audience, "If we could wave a magic wand, and overnight you could become absolutely excellent at any one skill, which one would most help you to double your income?" Then I have them write it down and discuss it. When they discuss these, the whole room goes wild. Everybody's laughing and talking, and laughing and talking.

Coming back, I say, "Let me point out two things. Number one, the great thing is all skills are learnable. Whatever skill you identify as helping you the most to double your income, you can learn. Everybody who has that skill today at one time did not have it. Number two, you're probably only one skill away from doubling your income, and now you know what it is. So write it down as a goal, make a plan, organize the plan, take the first step, and work on it every day. There's nothing that can stop you from achieving the greatness for which you were designed."

Dan

Brian, I've learned a lot. I want to encourage everybody—don't just read this book one time. Read it over and over and over again. Repetition is the mother of skill. And best of success to you.

INDEX